Artist: Francine Auger

Phyllis Munday, 1894-1990.

Kathryn Bridge

Kathryn Bridge has a master's degree in History from the University of Victoria and is an archivist and manager at the British Columbia Archives. She recently was the curator of the popular exhibition, "Emily Carr: Eccentric, Artist, Author, Genius" at the Royal B.C. Museum.

Bridge has written two previous books about women in B.C. history: *Henry & Self: The Private Life of Sarah Lindley Crease 1826 – 1922* (Sono Nis, 1996) and *By Snowshoe, Buckboard and Steamer: Women of the Frontier* (Sono Nis, 1998). The latter book won the Lieutenant Governor's Award for Historical Writing, 1998 and was runner-up for the VanCity Book Prize, 1999.

Kathryn Bridge lives with her family in Victoria and enjoys camping, hiking, and other outdoor pursuits.

THE QUEST LIBRARY
is edited by
Rhonda Bailey

The Editorial Board is composed of
Lynne Bowen
Janet Lunn
T.F. Rigelhof

Editorial correspondence:
Rhonda Bailey, Editorial Director
XYZ Publishing
P.O. Box 250
Lantzville BC
V0R 2H0
E-mail: xyzed@telus.net

In the same collection

Ven Begamudré, *Isaac Brock: Larger Than Life*.

Lynne Bowen, *Robert Dunsmuir: Laird of the Mines*.

Kate Braid, *Emily Carr: Rebel Artist*.

William Chalmers, *George Mercer Dawson: Geologist, Scientist, Explorer*.

Judith Fitzgerald, *Marshall McLuhan: Wise Guy*.

Stephen Eaton Hume, *Frederick Banting: Hero, Healer, Artist*.

Naïm Kattan, *A.M. Klein: Poet and Prophet*.

Betty Keller, *Pauline Johnson: First Aboriginal Voice of Canada*.

Michelle Labrèche-Larouche, *Emma Albani: International Star*.

Dave Margoshes, *Tommy Douglas: Building the New Society*.

Raymond Plante, *Jacques Plante: Behind the Mask*.

T.F. Rigelhof, *George Grant: Redefining Canada*.

Arthur Slade, *John Diefenbaker: An Appointment with Destiny*.

Roderick Stewart, *Wilfrid Laurier: A Pledge for Canada*.

John Wilson, *John Franklin: Traveller on Undiscovered Seas*.

John Wilson, *Norman Bethune: A Life of Passionate Conviction*.

Rachel Wyatt, *Agnes Macphail: Champion of the Underdog*.

Phyllis Munday

Canadian Cataloguing in Publication Data

Bridge, Kathryn Anne, 1955-

    Phyllis Munday: mountaineer

    (The Quest Library ; 18)
    Includes bibliographical references and index.

    ISBN 1-894852-01-X

    1. Munday, Phyllis. 2. Robson, Mount (B.C.) – Description and travel. 3. Waddington, Mount (B.C.) – Description and travel. 4. Lone Guiding Movement – History. 5. Mountaineers – Canada – Biography. I. Title. II. Series: Quest library; 18.

GV199.92.M86B74 2002   796.52'2092   C2002-940973-X

Legal Deposit: Third quarter 2002
National Library of Canada
Bibliothèque nationale du Québec

XYZ Publishing acknowledges the support of The Quest Library project by the Canadian Studies Program and the Book Publishing Industry Development Program (BPIDP) of the Department of Canadian Heritage. The opinions expressed do not necessarily reflect the views of the Government of Canada.

The publishers further acknowledge the financial support our publishing program receives from The Canada Council for the Arts, the ministère de la Culture et des Communications du Québec, and the Société de développement des entreprises culturelles.

Chronology: Lynne Bowen
Index: Darcy Dunton
Layout: Édiscript enr.
Cover design: Zirval Design
Cover illustration: Francine Auger
Photo research: Kathryn Bridge

Printed and bound in Canada

XYZ Publishing
1781 Saint Hubert Street
Montreal, Quebec   H2L 3Z1
Tel: (514) 525-2170
Fax: (514) 525-7537
E-mail: xyzed@mlink.net
Web site: www.xyzedit.com

KATHRYN BRIDGE

MUNDAY

Phyllis

MOUNTAINEER

THE QUEST LIBRARY

Publishing

For Art and Yvonne Bridge
and memories of Mount Revelstoke

Contents

Preface

I first "met" Phyllis Munday when Phyl's daughter, Edith Wickham, deposited her parents' records in the BC Archives, some fifteen years ago. As I worked to organize, sort, and inventory the photos and albums, what struck me most intensely were the thousands of powerful photographic images – panoramic views of jagged snowcapped peaks and icy glacier valleys, carefully annotated and labelled. This was my introduction to the majestic world of Mount Waddington, and to the Mundays' pioneering exploration into the heart of the Coast Mountains. Later, I included Phyllis Munday in two separate archival exhibitions that I researched and created, but several more years passed before I had the opportunity to undertake extensive research in preparation for writing this book.

ᴄᴏ

Phyllis Munday left behind an extraordinary legacy. Her physical prowess legitimized her in the largely male world of mountain climbing and inspired generations of women to follow in her footsteps. The time she spent in the forests, on mountaintops, on glaciers, and in alpine meadows, convinced her that our world is precious. Through her gentle teachings about the wonders and beauties of this natural world she touched

"Taken at my front door," Grouse Mountain, 1924.
A confident Phyllis Munday poses for the camera
not long before her triumphant ascent of Mount Robson.

many. Girl Guides, mountaineers, and the general public all benefitted from her nature lectures. Phyl Munday was an inspiring public speaker especially when she gave "lantern slide" shows featuring her exquisite nature photography. She was more at home in the outdoors setting, where she never lost an opportunity to combine hiking with observations of nature. A spontaneous, hour-long, engrossing examination of a nurse log on the edge of a trail leading to the beach remains a cherished memory for one lucky Girl Guide.

Phyl took photos and kept diaries and wrote up some of her adventures. She was also interviewed several times by historians and mountain climbers. These records (combined with those created by her husband, Don, a professional writer and journalist) are rich, intimate, primary source materials that complement the public archival records.

Phyl's own words, as written in her diaries and other writings and spoken in her oral reminiscences and conversations taped during interviews in the 1970s, provided me with raw material, which I then refashioned within the dialogue and commentary in the book. Many descriptive details about Guide camp adventures, climbing, and family life are Phyl's own words. All I have done is place them in the present tense and integrate them into the story. Thus the book is a blending of historical facts and Phyl's own words.

Writing this book has been a great joy because of the process that combined examination of the archival records documenting Phyllis Munday's life with the opportunity to speak directly with many who knew and loved her.

Phyllis Munday on the moraine of the Franklin Glacier
carrying a 32-kilogram pack, 1927.

Prologue

On Top of the World

Austrian guide Conrad Kain pulled a red handker-chief from his hip pocket, lifted his felt fedora off his head, and wiped his brow. He then looked below to the first of the roped climbers who followed. *Of all the clients I have had in the last fifteen years, I'll remember this one*, he thought. *She is stronger than most men, and has a head on her shoulders. Didn't once panic when that American woman almost got us all killed. I owe her for that one; it could have been a disaster. I'm glad this honour is all her own.*

He then began to loop the hemp rope dangling from his waist, to gather the slack as his climbing com-panion – linked by this rope – moved up to join him.

Phyllis Munday negotiated the last few steep and brittle steps over the crumbling ice and stepped up beside him. It was 4:30 p.m. on 29 July 1924.

Kain held out his arms and clasped her hand in his own. He pumped an excited handshake. "There, Lady! Here is the top of Mount Robson! You are the first woman on this peak – the highest of the Rocky Mountains."

Phyl's exhaustion disappeared and her face was transformed by a huge smile as she responded to the man's enthusiastic gesture.

"Now Conrad, *stop* before my arm falls off!" She reached up and removed her snow glasses from her face. The thirteen-hour climb from high-camp vanished from her thoughts. Here she stood on this narrowest ridge of broken ice covered with snow. She was 3954 metres above sea level. Here, nothing around her was higher – only air.

She took a deep breath of ice-chilled air. Soon it would be time to let the others have their time on the summit. But for now, it was all her own. She quickly thrust thoughts of the arduous ascent to the back of her mind. It had been harrowing and full of challenges, but there would be plenty of time to go over all those events later. This moment – now – here on the summit was for her alone.

The summit of Mount Robson was a great wind-driven snow cornice – capping the highest exposed rock on the mountain but projecting out and over it, without support. The narrow summit ridge was broken ice covered with snow. It was brittle and very steep, suitable for only one person at a time. Footsteps broke away bits of snow and ice and made each movement risky on this fragile surface. An avalanche here would shoot them all to certain death down one thousand metres, then over an enormous cliff of ice to the lower glacier.

Soon she would have to move back to allow her two other rope companions their turn. Her husband Don, with the second rope party, huddled some fifteen metres below her in the shelter of another great cornice. These four climbers also patiently awaited their turn on the top.

Phyl thought of Don and knew he would be wondering if she had yet made the top. She then focussed her vision beyond his resting spot and down even farther, studying the scene far below her. Her eyes travelled swiftly over the icy slopes that were dwarfed and somehow less daunting from this perspective.

Phyl looked down both sides of the mountain. To the north she could see Berg Lake almost three kilometres straight down, and over to the south in Robson Pass she could see the main-camp tents, which appeared to be mere specks. The comfort of "home" was a long way off. She lifted her gaze upwards, across the horizon, where range upon range of white, shimmering mountains spread out beneath her, beckoning, tempting. In any direction, for thousands and thousands of square kilometres, an unlimited vista of mountains, glaciers, snowfields, lakes, and waterways met her gaze.

Phyl savoured the moment – after all, it had been four years in the coming, four years of ambition and aspiration. She thought of all those climbs back home, the mountaineering adventures and challenges that had toned her body and prepared her mind for this ascent. She was the first woman up and a member of the third-ever party to make this climb. On the summit of Mount Robson in the Rocky Mountains, she stood five hundred metres above the highest point of any other mountain in the range. What a triumph! At this moment she was on top of the world, queen of all she surveyed. Unexpectedly, tears of emotion welled up.

No, she thought, *there's plenty of time for that. I only have a few minutes here at the top, and I have to record everything in my mind so I will always remember.* She willed the tears away and focussed instead on the majesty of the scene that lay before her.

"This moment is a four-year dream come true, Conrad. Thank you for leading us up." Kain smiled back. He too was delighted. He felt privileged to be back up on the mountain that had not been climbed since his own "first ascent" in 1913.

Turning slowly, Phyl looked down at her feet. There, stuck in the snow on the summit beside her, was a small film pack tab from Bert Pollard's camera. It looked so alien, so unnatural – brown and black nitrate against the white snow. But that is exactly why it was there. Pollard had made the ascent of the peak with Conrad Kain the previous day in the climbing party that returned to the high-camp with Kain while the Mundays awaited their turn. Bert Pollard had carried his camera to the peak to record the view and had placed the tab in the snow, where it would be seen by the next climbers and thus provide personal evidence of his own successful ascent. It is difficult to leave a permanent record on such a thin slice of mountaintop, for the constant grinding forces of wind, snow, and weather quickly sweep away any traces. Pollard knew that, but nevertheless it was a poignant gesture. Gently Phyl plucked the tab from the snow. She held it up for the guide to see, then turned it round and over before carefully resetting it up in the snow.

"There, that's my marker. Phyllis Beatrice James Munday was here!"

The hour was late, and their comrades awaited them just below the summit cornice. "I'm afraid that we cannot linger here on the summit," Kain remarked with an apologetic look on his face. "I must let the others have their turn and then we will all have to begin the descent before we run out of daylight. I don't fancy a night on the mountain, at least at this altitude! It's not stable up here – just look at the shifting snow – and the temperature will drop at least twenty degrees overnight." With that last remark, Kain held out the looped Beale rope to show Phyl. The rope was frozen stiff and hard, a testament to the coldness of the air, which Phyl had forgotten for the last few minutes, as she surveyed the scene from the summit.

There were eight climbers that day, four on each rope. Each would have their time at the top. Phyl moved off to allow the next two their turn. Ten minutes of pleasure and five of teeth chattering, that's how Kain described their brief reward on the summit. "A night out is hardly ever agreeable, and above 3000 metres, always a lottery," he commented. "We four must get down and let the others up. Time is now of the essence."

Twenty-one-year-old Phyllis James on the B.C. Mountaineering
Club trail up Grouse Mountain, ca 1916.

1

In the Wilds

M ountains – and the need to climb them – domi-
nated Phyllis Munday's life for almost as long as
she could remember. As a young girl she lived for a
time on Slocan Lake and also on a ruggedly treed hillside high above the western shores of Kootenay Lake,
about twenty kilometres northeast of the town of
Nelson, British Columbia. All around lay the Selkirk
Mountains, one of four parallel ranges in south-central
B.C. that form the Columbia Mountains.

On this rugged hillside Phyllis and her younger
sister Esmée lived with their parents Frank and
Beatrice James and baby brother Dick in a small, basic
house that in winter was nearly covered by snow.

Access was by either a rough cart track around the end
of the west arm of Kootenay Lake – which could take
some time, especially in winter when the deep snows
blocked the way – or by water. Travelling by water was
much easier, and even leisurely. Large paddlewheelers
and steamers such as the SS *Moyie* and the SS *City of
Ainsworth* operated on a regular schedule to serve the
people in settlements up and down the lake and to con-
nect the dozens of mining claims – like the Blue Bell
Mine at Riondel across on the east shore of the lake, or
here, where the James family lived near the Molly
Gibson Mine – to the urban centres like Nelson. The
steamers moved passengers, food, and machinery as
well as sacks of zinc, silver, and lead ore from the mines
to the barges and docks that were the terminus for the
small railways that then connected to the Canadian
Pacific Railway at towns like Revelstoke. Railways provided the transportation and communication links joining the Kootenays to the rest of the province, to
Canada and beyond. But travel, whether overland or by
water, all but ceased in the long winters of deep snow
and a frozen lake.

In this isolated spot in the Kootenays, Frank
James was employed as a bookkeeper. Family life here
was a dramatic contrast to their earlier brief residences
in Manitoba and England, but it was worlds away from
what it was in the British colony of Ceylon, (now the
country of Sri Lanka) an island just south and east of
India. Phyllis was born in the central hill country of
Ceylon on 24 September 1894. In Ceylon they had
lived as privileged colonists – English citizens occupy-
ing the upper ranks in the island's social strata. Frank

James managed tea plantations for the Lipton and Ridgeway companies. The family lived in the hill country on a tea plantation and enjoyed the comforts of colonial life that mirrored their social position. They were pampered, with servants to attend to the household responsibilities and nursemaids for Phyl and Esmée, who was known as Betty. The girls' mother, Beatrice, lived a life of leisure; she did not need to concern herself with cooking, cleaning, or many aspects of childcare.

Phyllis was only seven when the family moved from Ceylon in 1901, but these early days were imprinted on her memory. They gave Phyllis, in later life, an appreciation for her mother's strength of character, which allowed her to adapt from such a pampered existence to the one of self-reliance necessitated by Canadian living. Cooking, cleaning, planting and tending gardens, first aid, and other realities of rural domestic life all had to be learned and learned quickly. The Interior wet-belt of the Kootenays – heavily wooded with cedar, fir, hemlock, and birch trees – with its northern hemisphere climate of distinct seasons and dramatically cold winters, couldn't be more opposite to tropical Ceylon.

But the wild Kootenay country suited young Phyllis and her sister. Although the girls were quite young, here they were given a great deal of independence and freedom, in marked contrast to life in Ceylon, where servants were always present. Together they rambled and explored on their own, spending long days clambering along the hillsides. This tomboy existence was Phyllis's chief joy, but it was a concealed joy.

Her mother didn't always know exactly where they were on these rambles and would have been distressed to learn that Phyllis's favourite activity was to walk along the windfalls of trees across the ravines and deep gullies on the hillsides. She pretended to be a circus performer on a tightrope wire. These trees were fun to cross over by balancing along the trunk and scrambling over branches. The higher up the better. As Phyl became more proficient she challenged herself not to be frightened of heights and to focus on the act of balancing rather than the distance to the forest floor below. These skills in concentration and in footwork would be important for her later mountaineering expeditions.

∞

By late 1907 the isolated life and the irregularities of the mining concerns, combined with the fact that Frank James was in his late fifties and wishing to lead a less strenuous lifestyle, prompted a decision to move away from the Kootenays. Evidently the family decided to emigrate to New Zealand. Perhaps this was an opportunity to return to a more temperate climate. At any rate, they packed their belongings and came by steamer across the west arm of Kootenay Lake to Nelson, then by train from Nelson to Nakusp. At Nakusp, a small settlement on Arrow Lake, they transferred to a steamer, travelling to the head of the lake and then on to Revelstoke, where they boarded the Canadian Pacific Railway passenger train to Vancouver. From here they planned to depart for New Zealand.

But Vancouver was as far as they got. Once in Vancouver, the employment opportunities for Phyl's father combined with the pull of the city amenities and the gorgeous urban setting proved too great to resist. Vancouver was in the midst of a boom period in both population and economy. In 1901 the population totalled about 27,000 but by 1911 grew to 100,400. The city sat between the north bank of the Fraser River and Burrard Inlet. Beyond lay the very edge of the Coast range of mountains. Forests led up away from the populated urban areas to hills and snowy peaks. To the south, the flat, rich delta land of the Fraser River offered some of the best agricultural opportunities in the province. It was an extremely beautiful spot. And it was a much more accommodating climate with mild winters and warm – but not overly hot – summers. The James family settled on Keefer Street near the Grandview area, and it was from here that Phyllis completed her schooling and made the connections that enabled her to develop a recreational interest in hiking and climbing.

She was thirteen years old when they arrived in Vancouver, and it didn't take long for Phyllis to miss the freedom she and Betty had in the Kootenays.

"Don't you wish," she sighed wistfully to her sister, "that we could just go out the back door and hitch a ride to the end of the road. We would be nearer the mountains then, and we could just find an old trail and follow it wherever it would go. If we got tired, that would be it for the day and we could come home."

"It is too far to the mountains from here." Betty replied. "And besides, Mum and Dad would never let us go off by ourselves like we did before. Maybe we could go to Stanley Park one day soon though."

∽

Stanley Park officially opened in 1888 as a city park intended to be both a natural preserve and a recreational space. It lies to the west of the downtown core of the city of Vancouver and stretches over four square kilometres to include old growth cedar and fir forest. It is bounded on three sides by ocean and beaches and is wild and largely undeveloped. In the early 1900s Stanley Park was a wonderful retreat for Vancouverites. Driveways ran through the middle of it and circled around "The Hollow Tree," an enormous western red cedar measuring almost thirty metres in diameter and estimated to be over 1000 years old. Automobiles, pedestrians, horseback riders but mainly cyclists crowded the park on weekends, touring to Brockton Point and Prospect Point, where teahouses catered to thirsty and hungry visitors. Stanley Park allowed the city dwellers to experience wildness, albeit close to home, and was one means for Phyllis to keep in touch with the outdoors.

"Phyllis, let's go to the tennis club on Saturday," her father reminded her mid-week. Frank Munday was glad that their move to Vancouver made it possible for him to take up tennis again. In Ceylon, he had been the colonial men's champion for the island but hadn't had much opportunity to play since then. Living on Kootenay Lake in the bush precluded the possibility of tennis courts or many organized recreational activities.

Once in Vancouver, though, Frank James applied for membership at the Brockton Point Tennis Club and soon became renowned as a veteran player. In 1907 he was fifty-eight years old and one of the more senior players at the club. He loved the sport and really wanted to make a champion out of his eldest daughter, who showed promise.

Phyl's natural agility, nimbleness, and strength quickly put her at an advantage playing amongst girls of her own age who were less active generally and had little awareness of the outdoors activities that contributed to Phyllis's athleticism. While Phyl had roamed the hillsides and scrambled up the slopes above Kootenay Lake, girls her age in Vancouver had participated in few athletic pursuits. Girls invariably wore skirts or dresses and shoes designed for indoor rather than outdoor hardiness. Swimming outdoors in the ocean was an acceptable seasonal pursuit, although modesty forbade bathing suits, and girls went in fully clothed. Not an easy way to learn to swim.

Horseback riding – sidesaddle of course – was also acceptable, as was rowing or sailing in English Bay. Exertion was discouraged, in part because of the difficulties perspiration presented for laundering clothes that required hand washing and careful ironing. Bicycles were just beginning to gain acceptance, but for women and girls, sitting astride the wheels and pedalling vigorously was difficult to do while wearing long skirts and petticoats.

"Sure, I'll come, Dad," said Phyllis. "But I really want to spend some of the weekend in the wilds. Will you take me?"

"We just went to Grouse Mountain a few weeks ago. Why do you want to go up there again? You've been already." Phyllis sighed. She had a feeling her dad wanted to make her a tennis champion too. But there was something about getting away often, "in the wilds" as the family called it, that appealed to her more than anything else. Even though she and her family had just recently spent the day and had a wonderful picnic on the sunny lower slopes of Grouse Mountain, she wanted to go again. Although she couldn't really articulate why, it was important to her that she get away from the city and go to the local hills, to the forests.

"It's a whole day's planning to go, Phyl," her dad explained, listing off their route, even though Phyllis knew exactly what it was. First they packed a picnic lunch. They filled glass jars with water and screwed the lids on snugly to prevent leaks, then carefully wrapped the jars in linen napkins to protect them from breakage. They prepared sandwiches of fresh bread spread with pickles and meats, added a few hard sweets to complete their feast, and packed everything into wicker picnic baskets or into a carefully rolled-up wool blanket.

Leaving the house, the family walked to the nearest streetcar stop to catch a trolley heading towards Columbia Avenue and the small ferry terminal on the shore of Burrard Inlet. The ferry carried foot passengers across Burrard Inlet to a small wharf on the North Shore. Disembarking from the ferry, the picnickers hiked to Lonsdale Avenue, one of only three arterial roads leading from the wharf. A streetcar that ran along Lonsdale helped a little bit with the journey. From the end of the streetcar line, the picnickers climbed the rest of the way by foot on woodland trails over hill and valley and along creek-beds up the mountain. It took over three hours' travel time each way, which meant that if they wanted to spend most of the day "in the wilds" they had to make an early start, and return home late in the evening.

North Vancouver Museum and Archives/5655.

In 1912, Phyllis James and her Girl Guide company climbed to the top of Grouse Mountain in their full dress uniform and raised the Union Jack flag. Phyl is on the right with her sister Esmée (Betty) beside her.

2

Learning by the Book

At church one spring Sunday in 1910 Phyllis discovered that the local boys had been offered an opportunity she thought should be available to girls as well. A troop of Boy Scouts was to be formed at St. James Church.

Boy Scouts, a brand-new movement for boys aged eleven to seventeen, was founded in England by Robert Baden-Powell. Scouting was intended to build character and self-reliance that would stay with boys throughout their adult life. Patriotic in nature and very British in outlook, Scouting quickly became a popular means to develop friendships and to be athletically active.

Meetings of the local Boy Scout troops were held
weekly, often after school or in the evening. Boys
learned and tested themselves in many practical
aspects as they worked towards proficiency in a number of areas, each formally tested to earn a badge.
Badges once earned were sewn on to the sleeves of the
Scout uniform. The main thrusts of scouting – the
camping and outdoor activities and the earning of
badges – proved attractive challenges not only to boys,
but also to many girls at the time. At the first national
rally in England in 1909, it came as a great shock to
Baden-Powell that a number of girls (registered using
their first initials not first names) had actually crashed
the organization. In response, Baden-Powell quickly
appealed to his older sister Agnes and asked her to
help form an equivalent movement for girls that they
then called Girl Guides.

By 1910 Girl Guides had begun in England.
Canada and the other Commonwealth countries would
not be far behind. But since neither Phyllis nor her
friends nor her mother knew about this development,
Phyl begged the boys' Scoutmaster, James McDougall,
to allow a Girl Scout troop to form. When he agreed,
she convinced her mother to sign on as Scout Mistress.
Now all she needed was a minimum of eight girls to
form a patrol. This was a very easy requirement, as
Phyl quickly recruited her sister and six others. Phyllis
appointed herself Acting Patrol Leader. According to
the Boy Scout regulations, at fifteen she was not yet old
enough to be a full Patrol Leader.

At first the troop had only these eight girls.
Quickly, through word of mouth and notices at Sunday

school, more girls signed up. The average age was between ten and twelve years. Phyl admonished each new recruit: "It is important that we work hard and learn. In time there will be lots of us, but for now we have to set the example so others will join us. We'll have fun in ways that girls haven't had before!"

After they had been running along quite happily for several months, the girls discovered that unbeknownst to them, an official female wing of the scouting movement indeed existed, and it was called Girl Guides. Not only that, but a company of Girl Guides had already been formed, and they met at the First Presbyterian Church in Vancouver. This group had officially registered as the 1st Vancouver Company. Quickly Phyl called a meeting of the Girl Scouts to discuss the situation. There wasn't really much to discuss because it made so much more sense to become part of an official girls' movement rather than to continue struggling on their own in a system made for boys.

Mrs. James filled out the paperwork for them and reminded her daughter: "Now you realize that we will have to give up our name. I know you are proud to be a member of the 1st Vancouver Troop, but because we are now registering as Guides, not Scouts, we have to take the next available company name."

"It's not fair," said Phyl, "Even though we got ourselves going first and have been ever so busy, we'll have to call ourselves the 2nd Vancouver Company."

"Don't worry, dear, it's only a name. Names are not important. It's what you do that counts. Believe you me, your energy and enthusiasm are more important than any name."

Initially the girls dressed in long, full, navy or white skirts with a white midi blouse and a sailor hat. A more serviceable tailored dark blue skirt and button-down army-style shirt accompanied by a broad-brimmed cotton hat soon replaced this outfit. On their belts the Girl Guides carried the all-important whistle, knife, and all manner of gadgets. Later, more formal protocols in regards to lanyards, neckties, hats, and placement of badges on their uniforms came in to effect.

Scouting for Boys, written by Baden-Powell, was the principal manual for the Boy Scouts, and for the first few years it also provided guidance for Girl Guides. The manual was especially focussed on badge proficiencies and in particular, on first aid. Soon, though, Agnes Baden-Powell adapted this book and titled it *The Handbook for Girl Guides: How Girls Can Help to Build up the Empire*. The book countered the parental worry that Guiding would make tomboys out of daughters, for it included not only the essential Boy Scout woodcraft training, but also training in housework and domestic science.

For girls and women, Guiding offered a socially acceptable base upon which traditional female roles could be broadened to embrace previously male-only pursuits. Because the entire Guiding movement was female, girls and women learned to organize and be self-sufficient, to be disciplined, and to undertake challenging and nontraditional roles. For many girls, Guiding was heaven-sent. The training and the achievement of goals gave the girls confidence and provided the means and opportunity to develop self-esteem and purpose.

The skills learned in Guiding were practical and applicable for the average young woman, but for Phyllis these skills became a means to her ends. Guiding became a cornerstone of her personal identification, and throughout her life she would give back to Girl Guides as much as she received.

∞

Phyl and the other Girl Guides followed faithfully "the book," as they referred to their manual. Basic first aid formed the core of many badges and was generally acknowledged as an important life skill. Phyl took this subject seriously; she learned much of it by reading just in advance of passing it on to her girls. The manual was a handy tool that gave structure to their learning. It included detail on bandaging; treating burns, cuts, and abrasions; and responding to more serious accidents and emergencies. But little else existed to complement the readings. The Canadian Red Cross and the St. John Ambulance Brigade, organizations that would in later years contribute much in the field of first aid and emergency response, were in their infancy in Vancouver. Phyl even taught her girls artificial respiration by reading from the manual. At this point she decided enough was enough.

"Mother, how can I continue to do this? I can't possibly keep reading so far ahead of the girls to know enough to teach them. It's just too hard. I don't feel confident that I understand it all and I don't have enough time to practise before it's time to teach the Guides. There must be a better way, or else I will have to step down."

"Phyl, you always insist on doing everything yourself. It's an admirable trait, but once in a while you have to recognize that in some areas you, too, need a good grounding. Especially before you can expect to be a credible teacher. I think we should investigate some formal training. The St. John Brigade offers instruction. It may mean that you go to their headquarters on Saturday mornings for the next little while, but let's get you trained properly so you can pass on your first aid knowledge with some authority."

Phyllis nodded. Her mother was right, as usual. But also, as usual, Phyl followed through, and in September 1914 she earned her First Aid Certificate. Flushed with success, Phyl went on to earn the St. John Home Nursing Certificate three months later. First aid lessons for the Guides resumed once more. She continued using the Guide manual as a textbook, but now her teaching was based on confidence and the authority gained through her own formal certification.

"Read the chapter in 'the book' on bandaging," Phyl instructed the girls. "It is all covered there. We'll test ourselves next week when three of our mothers, who have agreed to come in, will make themselves available to us as victims. We can practise on them and try out all the bandaging skills we have worked on."

Phyl soon learned that "the book," despite its thoroughness on the subject of first aid, had limitations. In the area of woodcraft (knowing how to survive in the outdoors, how to build fires, and what plants could be used for food, to make shelter), it failed. Although much attention was paid to the subject – the plants and natural materials described did not grow on Canada's West Coast.

"Oh, this is hopeless! Mother, look. How can I learn when 'the book' is filled with English examples? If we study all this, we will know how to get food and shelter in the woods in England, but be hopeless at home. There is nothing here to guide us in the North American wilds. None of the berries or edible plants illustrated in 'the book' grow here in Vancouver. The trees are different, and there is absolutely no mention of salal, stinging nettles, Douglas fir, or cedar trees. Bears and cougars – important animals to know about if you are in the wilds – are not even acknowledged. Badgers, foxes, and rabbits do not populate my woods!"

"Then use all the resources available to you," her mother advised. "Where would you normally go to do research?"

"The public library, of course! That's being resourceful. As a Girl Guide, I should have been resourceful on my own, without you prompting me. Thanks Mum, that's exactly what I'll do."

The English Scouting books soon became the beginning – not the entirety – of the Girl Guide learning. Phyl and the others borrowed books from the public library and read about North American nature, about local animals, plants, trees, and geographic features. Phyl learned creativity and adaptability and how to apply general knowledge to specific situations, a life skill important for the unexpected and often unforeseen circumstances in which she sometimes later found herself.

Patrol leader Phyllis James, ca 1912-15.

3

Passionate About Guiding

Phyl's Guide company spent time in the outdoors on picnics and camping. North Vancouver was a popular destination for them because from the Grandview area it was relatively easy to get to – just a ferry ride across Burrard Inlet – and it was physically on the edge of "the wilds." The Grand Boulevard leading off Lonsdale Avenue was largely wooded and a perfect picnic destination. In fact, the whole of North Vancouver was rural with only a few key roads (with streetcar routes) cut through the forests. Besides the Lonsdale line, another line followed west along Keith Road to the Capilano River and another up the Grand Boulevard to Lynn Valley Road. North Vancouver was incorporated in 1907, but apart from these principal roads that had been laid out through the forests, little residential development existed until well into the 1930s. Grouse Mountain, Mount Seymour, the upper Capilano River, and Lynn and Seymour Creeks, along with many areas that today form part of the Greater Vancouver watershed, existed as wild, undeveloped forest land.

When Miss Elsie Carr, a member of the B.C. Mountaineering Club, became a lieutenant for Phyl's company, she introduced Phyl and the Guides to organized hiking. Under her direction the Guides undertook more extensive hikes along the lower Lynn Creek and on Seymour Creek. In 1912 they climbed – in their full dress uniform – to the very top of Grouse Mountain and raised the Union Jack flag, as if to claim the mountain as theirs. Phyl recorded the event with her Brownie box camera. At the Bowen Island Guide camp, Miss Carr took several of the Guides up Mount Gardner (elevation 767 metres). For Phyllis, Elsie Carr was an important role model.

Meanwhile, Frank James abandoned all hope of his daughter ever becoming a conventional athlete. She loved tennis, as she told him, "but I love the mountains best." In reply to her father's habitual question: "You've climbed one mountain, why do you want to climb more?" Phyl answered, "You've played more than one game of tennis on the same court. Isn't it the same thing?"

No doubt about it, Phyllis James was a bit of a misfit. Beatrice James didn't know what to make of her eldest daughter, who remained an outdoorsy, tomboyish girl despite her mother's instruction in cooking, sewing, and the other traditional feminine skills. But Beatrice remained ever supportive. As Phyl matured, she came to appreciate fully her mother's organizational skills and her behind-the-scenes work in both Girl Guides and charitable endeavours. Beatrice James was also a role model, not for Phyl's physical exploits, but for how to organize oneself and to be self-sufficient in practical life skills. All those cooking and sewing lessons came in handy.

In the days before the First World War, young women, even Guides, did not often spend much time in the hills and forests, so the opportunities to climb the local hills – with an appropriate chaperone such as Elsie Carr – were precious. The Guides hiked in long, heavy serge skirts, often to the ankle, stockings and eyelet-laced boots or street shoes, generally with slippery leather soles. They carried wool blankets or sweaters and wore wide-brimmed hats to protect their faces from the sun and weather. Their clothing was cumbersome to hike in, especially when breaking trail or exploring in the bush, and it was not water-resistant. But none of this mattered to a teenaged girl who came alive when walking in the woods, away from the conventions and social expectations of life in the urban setting of Vancouver.

∽

Early one morning in May 1913 Phyl and her Girl Guides, together with the St. James' Boy Scout troop, marched in formation to the B.C. Electric Railway station and boarded the train for New Westminster. What excitement! The Guides and Scouts wore their uniforms proudly. They were scheduled to march with their company colours in New Westminster's Empire Day parade. Each girl carried a pack with a lunch, for it was to be an all-day excursion. Phyl tickled with pride as she noted the girls in step with the boys. It was three years since those first meetings in the church basement. So much had happened since.

In the staging grounds amid the decorations, marching bands, and clowns, Phyl and the Guides did a double-take, for there, across the grassy field, came another group of girls, in uniform just like themselves. As the two groups of Guides spotted each other, excitement overcame them and they waved to each other in acknowledgement. Phyl stepped up to their leader, who looked just about the same age as she was, and introduced herself.

"Hello. What a wonderful surprise this is! I'm Lieutenant Phyllis James and this is the 2nd Vancouver Company."

"Hello back!" came the answer, "I'm Amy Leigh and this is the 1st Burnaby Company. Say, this is fun, we've never met any other Guides! We never knew that you would be here today."

The two young women compared stories and found that they had much in common, including a love of the outdoors. Amy was fifteen years old when she too became a patrol leader by default. Like Phyl, she was passionate about Guiding and took on an early leadership role. Now that the two Lieutenants met, they schemed to organize activities for both companies.

The Guides worked towards earning badges for proficiency demonstrated in a variety of specialities including the more traditional gender-based skills such as Cooking, Sewing, Laundress, Child's Nurse, Hospital Nurse, Florist, and Needlewoman. Athletics was an important component of Guiding. Badges to be earned included Swimming, Cycling, Gymnastics, Boatswain, and Horsewoman. Outdoors abilities led to badges for Naturalist, Pathfinder, Pioneer, Rifle Shot and to such nontraditional skills as Interpreter, Ambulance, Fire Brigade Work, Electrician, Telegrapher, and Signaller. The badges reflected the goal of the Girl Guide movement to make girls useful and self-reliant, and to develop those qualities of character that make good women and good citizens.

The First World War brought changes in daily life, but Guides adapted. Like many civilians and service groups, Guides were passionate about "war work," the volunteer labour devoted to works intended to aid the soldiers fighting on the front lines in Europe. In this "war to end all wars," Canadian soldiers, sailors, and airmen fought alongside their "Allies," the English, French, Russians, and others, against the aggressive German forces that threatened to take control of Europe. On the home front, the Guides contributed their part to the war effort and embarked on sewing and knitting projects to provide warm winter scarves, hats, mittens, and socks for soldiers fighting in the trenches of France. They sold candy and home baking, collected paper and postage stamps, and took on many other war relief projects. Enormous quantities of both second-hand and new winter clothing and shoes collected by Guides during the war years made their way to England for civilian use.

Each Christmas Phyl's company volunteered to sponsor one or two families, often soldier families. The Guides thought of everything the family might need for the festive season and went ahead, planning and organizing until all the little details were taken care of. They purchased a turkey from the butcher and bought vegetables and made plum pudding. The Guides also coordinated donations of special items for gift hampers and collected fruits, candies, nuts, and toys for the children. One Christmas the company sponsored a family whose mother was ill and away in hospital. The Guides cleaned and decorated the home, entertained the young children, and also cooked the family's Christmas dinner.

One of the earliest locations for Guide camps was on Bowen Island, in Howe Sound just off West Vancouver. Fifty-six square kilometres in size, Bowen Island was just far enough away from urban Vancouver to remain rustic and undeveloped. The island was a perfect retreat for Girl Guides because it was not too far for them to travel, yet it felt isolated. By the early 1900s coastal steamer ships regularly plied the waters between Bowen and the mainland. The Guides walked on to the steamer as foot passengers. They carried all their supplies with them and sometimes were so loaded up it was amazing to witness. At the Bowen terminal they marched off the ship, along the pier, and up the single-lane dirt road that wound away from the water.

The Guide camps on the island began quite modestly. Initially only a handful of happy, enthusiastic, and untrained girls shifted for themselves. It was remarkably unstructured. For many of the Guides, Bowen Island was their first introduction to living in the outdoors and they didn't know what to expect or what they might need to take with them. So each brought what she thought would be needed, and everyone shared food and tents. Luckily the weather was generally fair, and the food, although it lacked variety, kept them filled and happy. There was no cook, no nurse, no lifeguard, no formal organization at all – just girls who bravely ventured out on their own. In 1910, at fifteen years of age the oldest in her company, Phyl undertook responsibility for the girls on their first camping trip.

Eventually the Vancouver District Committee of the Girl Guides assumed organization of the camps and assigned each company a specific two weeks for their camping experience. In 1916 the *Vancouver Province*, in its regular Girl Guides column on the social page, reported on the arrangements for the camping season and listed the camp days assigned to each company. This year, the *Province* stated, "each girl would learn to row a boat." As the organization of the camps became more sophisticated, the campers' experiences changed from just rough-and-ready living to structured days and opportunities to learn new skills for badges.

The Burnaby Company, as Phyl learned, was very industrious and prepared everything from scratch. Amy Leigh told Phyl about how her Guides purchased second-hand canvas fabric to make their own tents. They drew paper template patterns for the roof, sides, ends, and door flaps, then placed them on the heavy canvas and cut the patterns into the fabric. It was difficult work that required sharp knives. They then tacked the canvas together with loose basting stitches and took these pieces to a local shoemaker, who double-stitched the pieces together and cut eyelets in the fabric for the ropes that, when anchored in the ground, would hold the tent sides taut and support it. The tents required uprights and a ridgepole for assembly, so at each site, the Guides cut down saplings to make these poles. "Doing it yourself" was to become a basic precept for Phyl in her mountaineering days. Camping equipment was too expensive and scarce to come by, so everyone just created home-made solutions.

The Guides packed all their food in with them, and each year they learned a little more about what quantities and varieties of foods worked best, were within a budget, and could withstand the time out-doors. One never could predict the weather. It could be cool, and therefore the milk might not curdle before camp ended, or it could be hot, without a breath of air, and meat would putrefy. Camping taught the girls to adapt to all aspects of living outdoors. Perishables such as butter, milk, and eggs they kept cool by placing them first in boxes, and then wedging the boxes safely in the stream by piling rocks around them. The meats, fruits, and vegetables they kept in larders – mosquito netted platforms – suspended in the air by ropes anchored over tree limbs, out of reach of animals and insects.

The Guides dug their own latrines in the forest soil, often making stick fences to create privacy; they also dug grease pits to receive grey water from cooking and washing. Over the grease pit they lashed stripped branches together to form a woven grid supporting freshly cut bracken fronds. As the grey water was poured onto the bracken, the ferns caught any errant spoons or solid pieces when the liquid passed through the fronds and down into the pit. The Guides then retrieved the spoons (important implements for their daily porridge) and buried the solid pieces to avoid attracting rodents.

At camp the girls divided into groups of six to a tent, and each group was responsible for the good order of their tent and campsite. The canvas tents did not have floors, so it was important that they be tightly pitched on a well-drained site in case of rain. The Guides dug trenches following the perimeter drip line to take away run-off rainwater from the sloping canvas roof. They created wash areas behind each tent by building camp furniture of sticks lashed together with twine. Rickety tables held enamel bowls for face-washing, teeth-brushing, or laundry. Pocket mirrors hung suspended from forked twigs, and towels flapped in the breeze from clotheslines stretched between trees.

Part of the fun for girls at Guide Camp was creating their own special home-away-from-home. Competition was fierce as the tents underwent daily inspection by the leaders, who gave marks for cleanliness and good order of the sleeping bags, clothing, and personal items in the tents. Guides swept the platforms or dirt floors of the tents, straightened guy-wires and tent posts, and rolled the tent flaps with precision.

Inevitably each Guide camp had its own special dynamics and events. One year the girls experienced an unwanted tension when a nearby farmer's field became home to Boy Scouts camping for the week. Not only was mischief in the air, but the girls felt they had lost their privacy and freedom. Having Boy Scouts camped so close managed to spoil the spontaneity at Guide camp because there was always just the chance that the boys might be watching.

Above all, Guide camps stressed real camping. Phyl bragged to some friends: "You know we don't wear white shoes and fancy dresses, we live and work hard in the wilds. You can't imagine how free it feels to sleep on a dirt floor under a canvas tent, warm and cosy, hearing the rain as it bounces off the canvas and slides down into the trenches. We stay warm and cosy because we know all about pitching tents and keeping dry. We are prepared as Guides should always be."

Understanding the environment and learning wood-lore was an important part of Guide camp, but not all Guides felt as comfortable camping as Phyl and her friends did. Camp could also be a time for fears and for homesickness. Night was difficult for some girls who missed their homes and families and felt that the days until camp closure seemed to stretch on forever. At times girls consoled a weepy tent-mate, snuggling closer for companionship and security. One night, as a girl moved closer to her friend who had woken with a nightmare, she slid her arm beneath her friend's pillow and to her surprise, she encountered a cold metal object. Curious, she asked, "What's this?" only to be told, "It's my revolver. Don't touch it! It's loaded and might go off. I've got it in case of bears. Mama said I should always keep the gun under my pillow for protection. Don't tell Captain, please! She'll think I'm a ninny for being scared."

∽

Guide camp was also a time to test oneself physically. Swimming was an important activity for the girls, many of whom did not regularly swim. In 1914 at the Bowen Island camp Phyl won her Swimming badge. She did this by swimming within a specified time a distance of over fifty metres wearing what was considered appropriate swimming garb of the day, a brown serge skirt with a huge hem down to her ankles. Manoeuvring in the water with such a heavy, clinging fabric around her legs was a challenge. The fact that the swim took place not in a warm island lake but in cold ocean water with a tidal pull made her accomplishment even more impressive.

At her first camp, Phyllis was already a leader both by virtue of her age and position as she moved from acting patrol leader to patrol leader. She later became an acting lieutenant and then lieutenant, and in 1915, a few months before her twenty-first birthday, she was granted a warrant certifying her as captain.

Beatrice James supported her daughters' Guiding activities in many ways. She herself was not athletic, but Beatrice believed that Guiding offered both her daughters unique ways to prepare for life and to develop independence of spirit. She remained active for several years on the Ladies' Committee for the Vancouver District. This committee supervised and encouraged the movement generally within the district, nominated suitable persons to act as captains, registered all companies and patrols at headquarters office in Toronto, and was responsible for granting of all badges and awards issued by headquarters. This committee also had the power to suspend officers or disqualify any company, patrol, or Guide in certain cases. In short, the Ladies' Committee was the interface between local and national, and the regulatory overseeing body for the district. Later, as Phyl entered adulthood and undertook more administrative work with Guiding, Beatrice continued her support.

4

*People Who Like
to Climb Mountains*

O ne afternoon Phyl had her arms deep into a medical supply cabinet as she hunted for iodine and rubbing alcohol. A cheery voice hailed her from out in the hallway.

"Phyl, are you in there?"

"Yes, I am. Is that you, Nina?"

"Of course it is – who else would come searching for you at tea-time?"

"I'll be right out, just hold on a sec…" Grabbing the last of the supplies, Phyl placed them on the wheeled cart and pushed it out toward the hallway. As she shut the door behind her and turned out the light,

Phyl and friends on the trail, ca 1916-18.

she pulled a key on a chain from the depths of a large pocket, and locked the door.

"All set. I could do with a cup of tea; I've been swept off my feet today. If it hasn't been one thing, it's been another. I never thought I would be filling in for the supply clerk when I accepted this posting."

"I know how you feel, Phyl. I've just been assigned two new patients in addition to my regulars."

"How do you keep up, Nina? So many patients and you only have one pair of hands. Surely your fingers must feel like they're falling off by the end of your shift."

"It's not so much my fingers, Phyl. Massage requires a tremendous amount of lifting and moving patients' limbs, or what's left of them in some cases. It's my arms – and my back – that really ache after a busy day. But, oh, nursing is good work and so necessary. These soldier boys have done so much for us. And now it's up to us to do what we can to help them back. For you and me, and all of us working here, it's the least we can do."

"I know," sighed Phyl. "I wanted so desperately to go overseas myself, but things just didn't work out." She pushed the cart up against the hall wall and hugged her friend with a big squeeze around the shoulders.

"Let's get that cup of tea. Maybe there will be biscuits left, but we had better hurry or those greedy-gusses will have eaten them and left not a nibble for us."

In the staff room, ten women sat in chairs in a circle, each holding a mug. They were nursing sisters and also administrative workers like Phyl, who worked in the orderly room as a stenographer.

"Well, you two – we had almost given up on you. Thought perhaps your watches needed winding."

"Phyl and I got to talking," Nina explained. "But thoughts of tea and your company were never far from our minds!"

Everyone laughed. It was so important to keep a sense of humour. Working at New Westminster's Royal Columbian Hospital, the nursing sisters like Nina and even the administration staff like Phyl, saw – unshielded – the after-effects of trench warfare on the human body. The military annex of the hospital was dedicated to veteran rehabilitation. Here, the shattered bodies of Vancouver's soldiers recuperated from grave injuries, illness, and psychological traumas inflicted by war. Many of the men had answered the call to arms in 1914 and headed overseas in October of that year as members of the 31,000-strong Canadian Expeditionary Force. Still others volunteered later; they left the West Coast and travelled via railway to Quebec City, then by troop ship across the Atlantic Ocean to Britain and the battlefields of France.

It was mid 1918 and the Great War was in its final months. In total, 55,750 British Columbians volunteered to fight. Some 6,225 never returned. Those that did return suffered greatly – from loss of limbs, loss of mobility or eyesight, the effects of privation and of poor nutrition, and exposure to mustard gas, the chemical weapon unleashed in the trenches on the Allied forces by the German army. Every man came home with memories and nightmares of unspeakable horror.

The hospital staff saw the veterans as they were, not putting on brave faces for their families, not masking the anguish as they tried to shut off the visions in their heads. The images of corpses rotting in the mud, of comrades crying out in pain and the relentless explosions of the guns and artillery were psychological horrors not easily treated by medicine. Rehabilitation of both body and soul was slow.

Phyl had a lot to offer. Her first aid and nurse's aide certificates did not allow her to work directly with the patients, but gave her an understanding of hospital procedure. After completing her schooling, she trained as a stenographer, learned shorthand so she could record dictation and then transcribe the shorthand into typewritten text. Her typing was excellent. She had no difficulty getting office work, but she preferred a hospital setting and had worked at Shaughnessy Military Hospital before coming to Royal Columbian.

∞

Now in her twenties, Phyl was occupied with her Guiding responsibilities after work a couple of evenings each week, and she had new duties with the Women's Volunteer Reserve, a service club training women for wartime service. The corps drilled at the police station and practised first aid. As it turned out, no member of the corps ever went overseas, but there was plenty of work for them to do at home, beginning with visiting returning soldiers at the local hospitals and fundraising.

But Phyl also had a new passion – the B.C. Mountaineering Club (BCMC), a locally based organization that began in 1907 as the Vancouver Mountaineering Club. Elsie Carr was a member as was

Phyl's friend from the Volunteer Reserve, Margaret (Peggy) Worsley. As soon as Phyl was twenty-one and old enough to apply for individual membership in the BCMC, she filled out the application form, which was then brought forward in October 1915 to a club executive meeting. Her sponsor and one other member vouched for Phyl's worthiness and she was admitted as a general member, which gave her access to club events, but not full or active membership. To be considered for active membership required not just an interest in hiking and climbing, but proficiency. The applicant had to climb two mountains (with appropriate club witnesses to verify) and also attend three club hikes. After quickly fulfilling all these conditions, two months later Phyl applied for active membership.

Just before the War, the BCMC boasted an active ninety members. One of the presidents later recalled the breadth of members' talents and variety of their backgrounds and occupations. He listed: "two lawyers, two land surveyors, three bankers, one botanist, two electricians, three salesmen, two railwaymen, two exporters, two nurses, seven stenographers, one meteorologist, three printers, one postman, one civil engineer, one cigar maker, one piano tuner, two real estate men – all gentlemen and gentlewomen."

Phyl soon volunteered her services, and at the March 1917 annual general meeting she agreed to stand for nomination both as a director on the executive committee and also for the club cabin committee. She was elected to the latter position. The following year Phyl was elected club librarian, a position she held for two terms.

The club leased land on Grouse Mountain and built a large cabin on it. The cabin, which was big enough to provide shelter for a number of hikers and to accommodate gear, food supplies, and cooking needs, became a weekend haunt for many members. Members using the cabin were asked to sign a guest book recording their visit and the dates, along with the names of visitors they brought with them. Phyl was very familiar with the cabin. Her first recorded visit was in August 1915 when Phyl and her brother Dick signed their names alongside that of her friend Peggy Worsley, who as club member authorized their visit. A few months later, after Phyl herself became a member, she began to bring her own friends and family to the cabin.

The club was egalitarian in nature and because it was relatively small and local, members didn't have to travel far afield as did those belonging to the Alpine Club of Canada, whose activities centred on the Rocky Mountains. The BCMC's regular weekend trips were inexpensive because everyone pooled their resources and shared food, and it was very informal. Beginning the trips on Saturday afternoon (after most office workers finished their shift) instead of in the morning allowed the majority of the members to attend.

Climbers were an unusual breed, and they kept their activities mostly to themselves and fellow climbers because in their experience the urban population had no interest in the outdoors and could not believe others desired to escape from the modern city and go to the hills. What attraction could there be to "set out into the wilderness" for no particular reason

– not to log, not to fish, not to clear land, not to build a road – but merely to enjoy the experience?

Hiking – the outdoors, the challenges, the wonderful variety and wonder in nature, the camaraderie of like-minded souls – was a tonic for Phyl. Fellow club member Neal Carter echoed Phyl's own feelings of delight to discover "that there was a whole Club of People who Liked to Climb Mountains; that They had a Cabin on the slopes of Grouse and Their Own Trail." Another club member penned a verse in the style of Robert Service and the closing lines summed up the feelings of those early climbers.

But say, comrade mine, isn't it fine,
Dog tired and loaded for fair,
To struggle back with a twisted pack,
And think of the joys up there.

Climbers like Phyl felt they could not survive without frequent opportunities to get out of the urban environment and retreat to the hills, to the snowy peaks of the mountains that surrounded Vancouver and extend north along the coast. Members climbed on all the local mountains – Grouse, Dam, Crown, Goat, Hollyburn, Cathedral, and The Lions. The club executive drew up a hiking schedule of regular weekend hikes and also the longer, three- or four-day trips. The trip director organized a rotation of members who each agreed to lead specific climbs.

Although the mountains surrounded the Vancouver suburbs, transportation to the extremities was limited. Each mountain required different access points. Once in North Vancouver, to go to Grouse Mountain (elevation 1211 metres), Phyl and her friends walked from the end of the Lonsdale streetcar line by trail. To go to Mount Seymour (elevation 1453 metres), the most easterly of the North Shore Mountains, they walked all the way from Lynn Valley. Some destinations required travel by B.C. Electric Railway interurban train into the Fraser Valley to get to areas like Golden Ears or the Chilliwack River and Mount Slesse (elevation 2375 metres) near the international border with the United States. The Lions (elevations 1599 and 1646 metres) northeast of the city, could be reached overland from Grouse Mountain or via the Howe Sound Crest Trail. A quicker way was to take a boat from English Bay or Horseshoe Bay and land on the beach at the foot of The Lions, then ascend straight from sea level. As her first big club climb, Phyl climbed the West Lion in 1916.

To get to the more distant peaks to the north, the club-chartered motor launch the *Tymack* left on scheduled Saturdays from pre-set locations at 2:30 p.m. precisely. The launch took the members closer to their climbing destinations by ocean, thus eliminating the time-consuming overland portions of the trip. Peaks such as Mount Tantalus (elevation 2603 metres) at the head of Howe Sound on the west side of the Squamish River, and Mount Garibaldi (elevation 2678 metres) sixty-five kilometres north of Vancouver, were not easily accessible.

Phyl met new friends in the BCMC, and many of these were young men. She and a girlfriend spent several happy afternoons joking with young men stationed at Point Grey to await their turn to head off to the battlefields of Europe. They played with the heliograph, a device for signalling by means of a movable mirror.

The mirror positioned at the correct angle to the sun created flashes of light beams visible over a distance. The flashes, either long or short – dots or dashes – using Morse code, allowed Phyl and her friends to send silly messages back and forth between the girls near the club cabin on Grouse Mountain and the boys at Point Grey. Another station was on the top of the Vancouver Building on Granville Street, so they had a triangle for signalling. It was a lot of fun.

Phyl was often at the club cabin with hiking friends Peggy Worsley or Margaret Lewis. She also brought her Girl Guides on summer weekends. In 1916 along with BCMC executive member P.J. Park, Phyl climbed up with soldiers on leave from the 62nd Battalion of the Canadian Expeditionary Force, then stationed locally awaiting their orders to mobilize and go overseas to the fighting.

In September of 1919 Phyl's Guides (between forty and fifty of them) travelled to Victoria on Vancouver Island to attend the first Provincial Rally, which was held in the Pemberton Woods near Oak Bay. Lady Barnard, wife of British Columbia's lieutenant-governor, was the Girl Guides' provincial president, and she took the salute to formally open the Rally. Each company spent a fun-filled competitive time showing off their skills in competitions to win the provincial pennant. The 2nd Vancouver Company and the 1st Burnaby Company together underwent formal inspection by His Royal Highness, the Prince of Wales.

5

Bloomers and Britches

"Phyl," began one of her colleagues at the hospital, "how can you be so perky at work every Monday when I know that you have been tramping in the bush and pushing your way through the forest climbing up some blasted mountain? Why aren't you exhausted?"

"Oh, it's not exhausting, I mean yes, it is exhausting, but it's exhilarating at the same time. It's hard work, but because it's hard, you feel so great when you've accomplished your goal. I never tire of that. Oh, I know I'm contradicting myself, but until you do it, you won't really understand how it can be."

Phyl James and Don Munday on the windswept summit of Mount Blanshard, 1918. Don poses with his camera while Phyl holds up a handkerchief to disguise her ripped clothing.

Don's first cabin on Dam Mountain. Here he and Phyllis stand beside the unfinished verandah, ca 1919-1922.

"I don't know if I'd ever want to do that – climb mountains, that is. I'd get all scratched and muddy and rip my skirts."

"We don't wear skirts. That would be nonsense. We would have to stay on nice, cleared trails and ramble ever so slowly if we dressed in skirts."

"But I've seen you on the streetcar on your way back home. Remember last month when you told me you had been up Mount Seymour?"

Phyl laughed. "Well," she said. "It's a better-kept secret than I thought. You don't honestly think we could get up the way we do and cut trails in a skirt? No, we start off from home in skirts but we always wear bloomers underneath. Some girls even wear britches underneath. Anyway, we can't be seen with anything like that, so we keep the skirts on over top until we're past civilization, where we can take them off and cache them under a log or something until we come back. Then the skirts go back on, and we're all ready for the streetcars and the ferry and for walking into the house."

"Well, that makes sense. I couldn't really figure out how you could do so much."

"You know the really funny part?"

"No."

"The worst thing is that when we cache our skirts, we lose our flexibility. We have to come back to the same spot at the end of the hike to collect them. Otherwise we can't get home! Did you know that it's against the ferry policy to allow women with bloomers on to the ferryboat? I've heard of a girl who had that happen to her. She came down at dusk, desperate to catch the last ferry from Lonsdale or else she would be stuck on the North Shore overnight and wouldn't be able to get home until the next day. Well, do you think she could find her skirt anywhere? She was running out of daylight and she came out of the bush a little west of where she went in, and in the failing light, she couldn't quite recall where she stashed it. She finally gave up and jumped on the streetcar to get to the ferry dock. But they wouldn't let her on the ferry. The purser told her that he was unable to accept her as a passenger unless she was appropriately dressed. So without her skirt, she lost her chance to get home that night!"

"That's hilarious. I can just see some poor girl who's miscalculated where she stashed her skirt turning over every rock and windfall desperately searching so she can run to the streetcar and not miss the last ferry. What a world we live in!"

"That never happened to me, but something really embarrassing did happen just a few weeks ago. We were on Dome[1], and it was a regular club hike. I was climbing over a great big log. It was on a slope, and a little bit off the ground, and as I got over it, the elastic in my bloomers got hooked on a snag and hung me up. There I was, suspended in the air, and I couldn't reach the ground. I was held up by the leg of my bloomers! Well, the boys all began to laugh, but eventually someone helped unhook me. I still haven't lived that one down. It will be a while yet until something equally embarrassing happens to someone else and I'll be out of the limelight."

1. Now called Mount Fromme, elevation 1175 metres.

☙

"Oh Phyl," said Nina, as the two young women walked down the hill towards their streetcar stop. Remember at tea break I mentioned my two new patients? Well, one of them seems like someone you should know. I asked him if he knew you, but he said 'No' he didn't, but that he had been away so long there were bound to be lots of new people in Vancouver."

"What's his name?"

"He told me his name was Don Munday. And he is a mountaineer! Just like you!"

"Don Munday – wow! He's almost a legend at the club. He's climbed all over Garibaldi and on Baker, and everywhere."

"Well, he was wounded at Passchendaele. It's a nasty one. A shell went clear through his left wrist and arm to the elbow. He won't be climbing any mountains for a while yet. He's got several more months of therapy – building up his strength. He's a brave man. Did I tell you also that he was given the Military Medal for valour during the Battle of the Triangle at Vimy Ridge? Say, shall I introduce you sometime?"

"Yes. I'd like to meet him, I've heard so much about him. I hear he's a little odd though – very intense. The way people speak, I've wondered if they are not just a little frightened."

One morning as Phyl worked at typing letters for the officer in command and patient reports for the matron from her shorthand notes, she heard a shuffling across the room and there, looking in the glass partition door, were Nina and a patient. The patient, a small man with closely cropped brown hair, hung a little behind her.

"Come on in," she gestured, signalling that it was all right to open the door and enter the office.

"Phyl, I've brought someone to meet you. It's his first really big excursion since surgery, but as he claims to be a great walker – what better therapy could there be than having to walk the length of the annex to the Orderly Room?"

Unconsciously Phyl's hand reached up to smooth back errant hair strands from her cheek. She smiled and rose to greet them. She pushed back the wooden office chair, then stretched across her desk and extended a hand.

"Hello, I'm Phyllis James. Nina mentioned that you were a new patient here. Pleased to meet you."

"Yes, Don Munday is my name."

"Although if you believe his charts, his name is Walter," interjected Nina.

"Oh, that is easily explainable," Don replied. "My complete name is Walter Alfred Don Munday, but when I registered for service, somehow they never got past my first name. Don will do. Pleased to meet you Miss James."

As they briefly shook hands, Phyl thought it was a shame he was so pale. His lower left arm and hand was swathed in bandages and immobilized by his side. He had obviously lost a lot of weight. His cheekbones protruded sharply. In contrast, his eyes sunk beneath his brow. His blue eyes looked straight at her. Phyl saw the same look she saw in all the vets: a guardedness and avoidance.

He is still a long way from recovery, she thought. *Physical wounds aside, he has the look of a lost man.*

"I've heard about you at the BCMC," she blurted out. "You'll have to tell me some time about climbing on Garibaldi. I haven't been yet – it's hard to get the extra days off work."

Phyl was extremely uncomfortable. Part of her was intensely curious to ask Don about the war and his wounds. She wondered if he would ever be able to climb again. The other part of her knew it was none of her business. There were so many men recuperating and each had his own horrible war memories. She was a little taken aback too. This small man didn't look strong enough to have done everything she had heard of him.

"Well, it seems I'll be here for a while yet, so maybe we'll meet up and you can fill me in on all the club news. How is Tommy Fyles?"

"As busy as ever. He is still organizing all the trips, and leading most of them as well. We have a system. Are you familiar with Dunne and Rundle's camera shop on Granville near Dunsmuir? Well, one of our members works there and they keep a special drawer in the shop just for the club. The weekend trips are all posted there. If you want to go on the weekend trip you go in and put your name down. Then they divide the names into messes, and you go back to find which mess you are in. It works out rather well. The list says what food you are responsible for bringing – enough for the four or five people in the mess. We all camp together and it's wonderful fun. But I expect you know that already."

"Well, I did most of my climbing with a few pals. We didn't go in for the big crowds. Sounds like hiking is pretty popular now."

During the summer of 1918 Munday continued his recuperation, which involved extensive massage and physiotherapy for his left arm and hand to repair the nerve and soft tissue damage. The ligaments and muscles required constant work, first re-establishing the gross motor movements and then the fine ones. As his arm healed, his general physical condition improved, and soon the two began to go for walks in the evening. Later he was well enough to walk with Phyl to the BCMC meetings in town.

Don talked, haltingly at first, of his war experiences. He had not wanted to go to war; in fact, he struggled with his conscience for some while, but the responsibility proved too great. On 27 June 1915 he climbed alone. This day was the day of decision. "As I stood on the snowy summit of Cathedral Mountain I found it very hard to renew my resolve to enlist until a strange coldness crept down over the mountains, as though their aspect declared, 'Unless you are worthy to make this sacrifice you are unworthy to frequent our shrines.'"

Two days later, Munday enlisted as a private with the Scout Division of the 47th Infantry Battalion. Scouting was a job that suited him well. His mountaineering background, his map reading and use of compass, and his other orienteering skills held him in good stead. A scout's business was to see that the men got to the places they were supposed to when they were at the Front and to get them back again. This meant

Munday had to "take their position" so he could find it again upon return. He had to know exactly where they were physically on the ordnance map and then "scout out" the area into which they had been ordered to advance, noting all the hazards, such as enemy gun emplacements and trenches. Then he had to guide the men forward to their destination, whether it be a visible geographic site such as a ridge or hill, or more likely than not, just another muddy indefinable spot in a sea of blasted land devoid of landmarks. Coming back from one of these ventures on 24 October 1917 at Passchendaele in Belgium, he was hit with a shell and wounded. Passchendaele, the last major offensive of the war, was also one of the most horrendous. In this battle alone, 15,654 Canadian soldiers were killed or injured. Munday, like so many others, was patched up on the battlefield and eventually shipped home.

Although repeated surgeries repaired much of the damage, he couldn't use his hand for all functions. He could not grip or pull his fingers together. In the early days of recuperation, what would be a lifetime disability was especially challenging for this man who was passionate about strenuous outdoors activities.

In August 1918 Munday was granted weekend leaves from Royal Columbian Hospital, and unbeknownst to the officer in command (O.C.) at the hospital he immediately commenced weekend hikes. He was still a patient at the hospital and not yet discharged from the army. Some of the nurses (and Phyl) knew his plans but chose not to distress the O.C., for it would certainly have meant trouble for all. As a matter of fact, Don's first major transgression on weekend leave was at the invitation of Phyl and Peggy Worsley. These two had earlier made an attempt to explore an area accessible from Alouette Lake but ran into logistical problems that they had not anticipated. Access to the area was dependent upon the good wishes of a power company gauge-reader stationed at the lake. He controlled the canoe and was reluctant to permit two unescorted young women into the area. Evidently he relented, but only late in the day. Phyl and her friend were unable to do more than reach the base of Mount Blanshard that weekend.

Well, they thought: *Why not invite someone we know, who happens to be male, as an escort?* Thus, Don Munday found himself tramping the shadowy trail along Alouette River, autumn leaves swirling and fluttering in the breeze. The three slept on the lakeshore in front of the gauge-reader's cabin, having successfully negotiated with him to carry them the next day by canoe across the lake. The hike took them westward to a ridge paralleling the lake, through heather and stunted alpine trees. On they went, and the afternoon was half spent before they began the ascent of Mount Blanshard (elevation 1706 metres). They believed that they would climb the reddish tooth of the summit and return before dusk. So confident were they that they only brought along with them a few scraps of chocolate and no lights. They left the remainder of the supplies in a camp struck on the heather. The climb was strenuous: steep cliffs covered with a good deal of matted growth – scarred, contorted tree trunks of subalpine conifers with trailing branches at knee height. Climbing over these wiry obstacles was not often practical, and struggling through was not only hard on their clothes but took more time than they realized. Don had his compass and always knew where they were, but travelling was a little different as they had to avoid difficult left-hand pitched routes because of Don's hand. He couldn't use it to full strength, and he was still in the midst of treatments. The three climbers finally got to the summit in time to see the sinking sun cast the shadow of the mountain in a slim violet wedge for miles across the forested fringes flanking the Fraser Valley.

But they made it. To prove their ascent – which was the first one recorded – they took photographs of themselves on the summit and built a rock cairn. Climbers left evidence of their ascent usually in the form of a signed and dated note with their names. This note was sometimes encased in a glass jar, or tin box, protected from the weather and placed beneath rocks on the summit. In this way, future climbers knew that others had preceded them. To pose for one of the photos, Phyl had to hold a handkerchief at a curious angle to cover the devastation to her clothing from the climb! Off with the packs, Phyl, Peggy, and Don slid to the ground and congratulated themselves on their efforts. They were not as fresh as they thought and yielded to the temptation to stay too long on top. By the time they began the descent, light had faded. There was no moon. In the darkness they could not distinguish one essential bit of the route, and it was soon unsafe to continue. The only place to spend the night where they would not be required to stand up was on a ledge just wide enough to sit upon with their legs dangling over the sharp edge above a long drop below.

Despite the uncomfortable positions, they slept. At first light they resumed their descent. The homeward tramp to get the last train developed into a dull grind. Phyl and Don saw Peggy Worsley off at her train stop outside Haney and exchanged weary goodbyes. The train continued its journey along the valley heading west. Rest was not possible. A weekend holiday crowd had made the train late, and it was packed with passengers. Phyl and Don had to stand in the jammed aisle, heavy packs on the floor between their legs. The train arrived late at the station, and they missed the last streetcar in New Westminster. Sore beyond belief, Phyl took her boots off and walked in her stocking feet. Don walked with the automatic movement of a soldier, but literally went to sleep on his feet, again and again. Not a single automobile was to be seen. No police patrol car (which might have stopped to question their clumsy movements and perhaps taken pity on them, or transported them back to the hospital). Ascending Mount Blanshard was not a wise weekend activity for a recuperating soldier, but it was typical of Munday: he continually pushed his limits and by example encouraged those around him to do the same.

6

Romance Above the Clouds

In the summer of 1919 Don and Phyl were on a club hike on Mount Baker in Washington State. There were three of them in a group, and they climbed with an air of confidence – they were not roped together. Midway on the ascent they encountered a section of moraine – the mass of loose rocks deposited by a glacier – on the edge of a steep, washed-out creek gully.

"Aahhh." Phyl was instantly on alert. The sound came from Don on the moraine above her. She moved instinctively and with remarkable speed. From her position on the upward slope Phyl sprang to place herself several metres below on a rock outcropping, and she braced herself for the impact. *He's going to go over*

Happy honeymooners. Don and Phyl snuggle together
"in the wilds," 1920.

the edge. Please God give me strength to hold on to him. Don's footing gave away completely and he was tossed out from the moraine slope. His body flipped over in mid-air above her. Phyl reached out to grab him and managed to pull his weight towards her, against the slope, in a desperate move to prevent his certain fall to the bottom of the gully. But just as his feet came down near her, the ground she was standing on broke away as well. As she held Don, Phyl began to lose her balance. Don clung to the rocks beside her and it was enough support to give her the moment or two she needed to rake out tiny ledges with her nailed boots.

"Are you stable?" Don asked. "I'm just hanging by a thread," Phyl replied, as she looked around for a more promising ledge. Together they scrambled away from the gully edge and crossed the moraine upward, towards their companion. Around the campfire that night Don told the story. "Phyl was a marvel. She seemed to know even before I did of the danger that I was into."

Instinctive action or not, Don was convinced that a bond of communication existed between the two of them that did not require audible language. And thus commenced Don's courtship. By nature, Don was taciturn, uncomfortable with extended conversation. His face held little expression, and it was difficult to read his thoughts. His outward appearance was the very opposite of Phyl's; her expressive face could bubble over with enthusiasm. But behind Don's façade was a romantic soul who composed poems about the beauties of nature and was a keen observer of all living things.

He had loved before and knew love's joys and pain. When he left for France he left also a relationship. While fighting in the trenches he had plenty of time to muse, but unfortunately, as he wrote, "my thoughts [alas] will return to where my heart is still." By the time he was back at home in Vancouver, Don was over this love, and then appeared Phyl, embodying in her love of mountains a reflection of his own self. She was the one for him! Phyl, however, was not immediately smitten with Don's personality. He was very different in character, she more spontaneous and outgoing, he more quiet and soft spoken, and he seemed so intense – but that was a characteristic shared by many men upon their return from war. She enjoyed his company and respected his abilities – he could teach her a lot about mountains and climbing. But, she insisted, she did not feel romantically inclined towards him. Phyl took a while to be persuaded by Don, who patiently bided his time. In the meantime they continued to hike on club-organized events and spent increasing amounts of time together.

When Munday finally completed treatment for his injury, he had not regained the complete use of his arm and hand. He was able to do many things, but certain movements, such as carving a roast or tying his shoelaces, remained difficult. He was forever to travel with a small ball of wadded paper in his pocket. At odd moments he would put his hand in his pocket and roll the paper to keep his fingers nimble.

Munday's army discharge came in the fall of 1918. Because of his injury he could not resume his previous work as a carpenter but concentrated instead on expanding his freelance writing career. Besides, the typewriter provided good physiotherapy for his injured arm and kept his fingers agile.

In his spare time, Munday served on the executive of the BCMC and for two years volunteered as the editor for the monthly newsletter, *The BC Mountaineer*. He also contributed much of the content. He wrote up accounts of climbs he, Phyl, and their friends undertook, many of which were first ascents, that is, the first documented climbs to the highest point on a mountain.

∞

On 4 February 1920 Phyllis Beatrice James married Walter Alfred Don Munday at Christ Church, Vancouver. Don's brother, Bert Munday, and Phyl's sister Betty McCallum (who herself had married a young soldier in 1914) stood as witnesses. The *Vancouver Province* reported the event in its social pages, noting: "the young couple are concluding a romance that started with mountaineering some years ago."

The day of the wedding was uncharacteristically foggy. Phyl had a small apartment on Walden Street in South Vancouver. It was not a long distance to the church, but given the weather, the bride-to-be arranged to leave the house for Christ Church an hour early. She was to be there in time for the service at nine o'clock that morning. The groom lived with his widowed mother on 29th Avenue East, just around the corner from Phyl. Despite the worry, everyone arrived on time. The ceremony was attended by many family members and friends, but immediately afterwards,

Phyl and Don – much to the chagrin of Beatrice James – exchanged their wedding clothes for hiking ones, picked up their packs, and headed off to catch the streetcar and then the eleven o'clock ferry to North Vancouver. They caught the Capilano streetcar to the end of the line and walked all the way from there over to the west ridge of Dam Mountain, where Don had just finished building a small cabin. Their idea of a honeymoon was to do what they loved best – live in the outdoors away from the city – and to do it together.

The weather was cold, but the cabin had a chimney, and soon a big fire kept the chill out. While Vancouver experienced a week of thick fog and drizzle, above the clouds the Mundays enjoyed clear, bright, glorious February weather. From the cabin they climbed somewhere different every day.

Building the cabin had been Don's own special therapy, but it made a romantic story at the time of his marriage and caught the imagination of the local press. Single-handedly he blazed a trail, then "every weekend and on holidays laboriously, and with the patience of an ant, stick by stick, stone by stone, piece of furniture by piece, he carried the makings and furnishings of a little hut up the steep mountainside to a cunningly concealed broad ledge with a wonderful outlook on the sea and land. Then he built a comfortable mountain retreat, thinking of the day when he would spend his honeymoon there."

In February 1920, a few weeks after their wedding, Phyl and Don decided to go to the Rockies for a mountaineering challenge. They had heard so much about these mountains from friends in the BCMC and felt confident in their abilities to climb farther afield. They loaded their supplies on to the Canadian National Railway car and travelled across the province to Mount Robson Provincial Park. Arranging for pack horses proved impossible so they carried their thirty-kilogram packs from the train station by trail to Berg Lake, where they camped. One might have thought that entering a new territory such as this in mid-winter without guides and relying only upon maps and Don's compass would be daunting. For the Mundays it was adventure. While ascending Lynx Mountain (elevation 3170 metres), they discovered that even the surefooted mountain goat could make a fatal misstep as they watched a young goat fall while climbing a cliff above them. Despite this sad event, the frequent glimpses of wildlife in this park made the biggest impact on their remembrances and were an important turning point in their views about game hunting. The camera would remain the Mundays' only means of hunting game and their only trophies would be photographic ones.

Phyl and Don Munday also climbed Resplendent Mountain (elevation 3426 metres), and not merely via the route established by legendary guide Conrad Kain in 1911. They pioneered a new route. A sudden weather change forced them to race for their lives to a rock rib when snow on an ice slope began avalanching. Lynx and Resplendent exceeded the elevations of any of the coastal mountains they had yet encountered, and these ascents gave them a taste for something more than what they were used to. Because of their elevations, both mountains presented more ice climbing than rock. Phyl liked climbing on snow and ice, because, as she put it, they are always changing. Rocks were fixed things, so rock scaling did not interest her. But the ever-changing conditions of snow and ice on high mountains created an unstable, evolving landscape and presented a mental challenge to find the best route as well as a physical challenge to withstand the conditions of cold, wind, and the dangerous natural obstacles created by glaciers and avalanches.

Phyl learned a tremendous amount on this 1920 trip to the Rockies. She now had firsthand knowledge of a new mountain paradise and wanted to become involved with the people who climbed there. Applying for membership in the Alpine Club of Canada (ACC) seemed the best way to do so, and together she and Don schemed to facilitate a trip to one of the fabled ACC summer camps in the Rockies.

She had also had the opportunity to see Don in action with his new boots. For years climbers wore leather boots with edge nails. Edge nails – a special type of steel nail with a long spike on it – were ordered in bulk, and then each climber applied them to the soles of the hiking boots by pushing them through the sole. The nails were then clipped over so that the two portions of the edge nail were just on the counter of the boot. Edge nails on the boot soles acted a bit like crampons, but unlike crampons, which were worn using bindings to fit them directly over the boots, these nails became part of the actual boot sole. Edge nails were particularly good on logs and slippery surfaces, but on the ice, they slipped.

Although Don had been wearing his new tricouni nails for a year, Phyl had remained unconvinced of their advantages. Tricounis were not easy to apply, and it was very important that they be pushed directly through the leather and not through pre-drilled holes. The prongs on the nails were so shaped that they spread when driven in and thus locked the nail securely. Only in the Rockies on the glaciers did tricounis really show an advantage. They did not slip on ice as did edge nails and could be worn equally well on rock. During this trip to Mount Robson Provincial Park Phyl came to believe that Don's boots gave him a big advantage, and she was finally convinced of the merits of tricouni nails. She decided then that she should also switch over, a decision she never regretted.

When Phyl married Don, she did what women of her age and time did, ceased to work and became a housewife. To keep herself occupied she threw herself into Guiding. The Company was now so large and doing so well that Phyl thought she should organize a ladies' committee to introduce other women, especially mothers of Guide-age girls, to the Guiding movement in a formal way by providing information and training as a means to encourage the creation of more companies. Dominion Headquarters appointed Mrs. T.P. Lake to be the very first commissioner for the Vancouver District. Her presence gave structure to the committee, which later came to be called the officers' council. Phyl was appointed Staff Captain for the district, and a secretary and treasurer were also named. The Guide Company split into two companies of reasonable size, each with its own leader. At the same time Phyl created the 1st Vancouver Brownie Pack, and she herself became their Brown Owl. Brownies, for girls aged seven to ten, was an offshoot of Girl Guides, introduced by Agnes Baden-Powell after much demand for a Guide-like organization suitable for younger girls. Brownies fed naturally into Guides, as did Guides into Rangers. Thus a girl could stay in the movement as she matured.

In the summer following her marriage, Phyl discovered that she would soon have her "own little Brownie." She was pregnant. As an expectant mother she now had a new role for which social conventions of the times remained quite rigid. Physical activity was discouraged. The doctor prescribed moderate exercise such as gentle walking, but he certainly could not endorse either the vigorous "walking" associated with mountain climbing or the strain of backpacking, which he viewed as potentially harmful to the unborn child and the mother-to-be. *I'm fine until the pregnancy shows*, thought Phyl. *Don and I will just continue as usual, perhaps with a little accommodation, we'll stick a little closer to home, until I can't hide my condition.*

Phyl continued on with the Guides until just a short time before the birth of her child. She applied for and was granted a seven-week leave of absence from Guiding, and during this leave, gave birth to Edith on 26 March 1921. Within a very short time, Phyl was up and about, little affected physically by the nine months of pregnancy and the labour and delivery of her child. In typical Phyl fashion, she quickly incorporated Edith into her outdoors adventures. The new baby did not deter Phyl and Don from hiking and climbing for long. When she was eight weeks old they began taking Edith to the cabin on weekends, and at eleven weeks Edith travelled up Crown Mountain (elevation 1503 metres) in a cotton sling around her Daddy's shoulder while Don steadied her head with his arm.

The *Vancouver Province* featured a large article complete with photos that showed the family on the summit of Crown Mountain. The Mundays and their new baby became celebrities. Vancouverites were captivated by the activities of this novel couple, who projected such a matter-of-fact outlook as they carried on as usual, seemingly little encumbered by the addition of an infant.

One day a few months after Edith's birth and after their climb up Crown Mountain, Phyl visited her mother and explained Don's latest invention. "Edith is growing like a weed. She is strong and she won't be content any longer to travel in the sling. So guess what, Mum? My clever husband has made a very nice little carrier for Edith. The carrier will fit right on to his packboard over top of a small load, and that way Don will be able to pack Edith in a much safer way. She'll like it too because it will give her a little more freedom to look around. The carrier has a wooden base with canvas on it and a big canvas band, so that when we put her into it, it holds her right around from her hips to under her armpits. It supports her firmly so that she doesn't slide down into it, and best of all we can put her in, fully dressed, and she'll be covered up with the canvas. That way we don't have to worry whether it rains. She won't get wet. Don has also made a hood to it, so that if it really rains we can pull it over her head. And then, mosquito netting. That will be ever so important in the summer."

A few days later on the first of July the Mundays packed right through the Seymour valley and down the Stawamus valley into Squamish with Edith. On the way they camped in one of the cabins of the Britannia Mining Company. The cabins were equipped with bunks and a stove for cooking. Phyl, ever resourceful, quickly saw a practical use for one of the monstrous big bread pans that the company cook used for baking. *What better bassinet for bathing my baby in the morning?* One day while they were still staying at the cabin, three geologists from the mine dropped in for a visit. They were absolutely stunned when they saw a small baby in a bread pan on the oven door.

Later in the same year Phyl and Don went into the Selkirk Mountains to the BCMC camp and took Edith along. It was just shortly before the old hotel at Glacier was closed, and the people there wouldn't believe there was a baby at camp up the valley. She was contented and seemed to enjoy being out like that, so Phyl and Don just brought Edith with them all the time. Had Phyl been less strongwilled about her love of the outdoors, and had Edith been less co-operative, the young mother would have had to give up her outdoor activities now that she had a child.

7

Rambling High on the Ridges

Phyl and Don, accompanied many times by Edith, spent the decades of the 1920s and 1930s in Phyl's words, "rambling high on the ridges." They were bounded by the routines of family, employment, and domestic responsibilities yet managed to set and keep as a priority this need they both shared to be in the mountains.

"My love for the mountains is terribly deep," Phyl wrote in her diary. "They mean so much. It is impossible to explain what they do to your soul. There is nothing on earth like them." On many weekends, and for longer opportunities in the spring and summer, the Mundays climbed in the lower mainland or the Tantalus

Phyl and three-year-old Edith outside Alpine Lodge, their home
on the Grouse Mountain plateau. Phyl packs chairs for the cabin
and ferns for the table setting, 1924.

and Britannia Ranges on the coast north of Vancouver, the Cheam Range south of the Fraser Valley, the Cariboo Mountains, and the Rockies. Before their marriage, Phyl at times had incurred the displeasure of her employer when she arrived late for work on Monday, or alternately, did not make it in until the next day. It was impossible to be sure about how long it might take for a weekend hike. Weather could change, transportation might cause delay, injury or accident was always possible. Phyl managed to convince her boss at Begg Motors that she really wasn't dallying with the time clock.

"The only boat we could get to rent was a yacht with a very deep keel. We went in on a high tide at Bishops Beach way up Indian Arm and of course, we didn't allow for the tide and we got stuck and couldn't get away again until the next high tide. That didn't get us back until the next morning, you see, the morning after we should have been back. So, I'm sorry, but that is why I missed a whole day's work."

Her boss had remained unconvinced. In his eyes, Phyl, nicely turned out in a smart suit for her office job, did not appear as he imagined a passionate mountain climber should look, especially one who claimed to have been marooned by the tides. He really believed she was making up the story.

"I'll bring you evidence to prove that I was mountain climbing," she had promised, hoping she would not be fired. "I'll show you the pictures. I can take the film in today at lunch and it should be ready later this week. Just please, let me stay here working until then, and then you will see. I don't mean to miss work, but sometimes the unexpected occurs."

The pictures backed up her story, and Phyl's boss had finally believed that she really had intended to get back on time, and had not just fabricated a wild story to get an extra day off.

Don earned a living as a freelance journalist and a writer. He had no boss to face on Monday morning, although manuscript deadlines and publication dates kept him on track.

∞

Phyl put her skills and experience on hold for several years and stayed at home to care for Edith. Yet Phyl's "at-home" life was not exactly traditional in routine. Taking advantage of what she called "the extra time" she now had as an at-home wife and mother, Phyl continued with BCMC activities, especially the social ones, and organized many club dances and parties. She undertook more and more responsibilities in Guiding and, as always, partnered with Don on outdoor ventures, in their leisure time "exploring and climbing in unknown mountainous parts of B.C., mapping, studying, and collecting specimens of insects and flora for the Provincial Museum in Victoria, as well as photographing and studying the snow and ice of the big glaciers."

∞

Women climbers in Phyl's day were accepted only if they kept up with the men and disguised from others the fact that they hiked. Phyl always thought it unfortunate that so many women were discouraged from pursuing climbing because they were not as strong as the men, and she advised women: "Don't go too fast at first. Just go steadily to begin with and do the breathing, in and out as regularly as you can, with the movement of your body. Have the right attitude and just hang on with it."

There had been some changes in women's clothing since Phyllis first began to hike and could wear hiking garb only on the mountain slopes, never below. Knickerbockers were a wonderful improvement over the bloomers that had been easy to hide under skirts but so voluminous they caught up on the bushes. Knickerbockers were tapered like a man's pant, but only came to the knee. Women could wear knee socks or tights underneath, although "puttees," a kind of khaki cloth wound round the legs below the knickers almost like a bandage from the knee to the boot, were most popular. Puttees were actually good for snow because they kept the snow from getting in your boots and were thus a precursor to gaiters. Britches – as Phyl called the first trousers worn by women – were held up by a pair of suspender straps. Eventually in the 1930s and 1940s women began to wear more tapered ski pants with an under-foot strap that held the pants tight to the body and prevented snow from getting under the legs of the pants.

The fabrics used in those early days were made from natural fibres, not synthetic. The first tents Phyl and her Girl Guides used were a heavy canvas that was firm and stiff and very water repellent. The canvas was perfect for a fixed camp location but not at all suitable for packing and taking on the trail. For backpacking in to the bush and on climbing expeditions, Phyl sewed their tents of sail-silk or Egyptian cotton, a light, tightly woven cloth that had proven to be durable in wind and rain. Don designed the tents and made templates for all the pieces. Then they shifted the furniture out of their living room, laid out the fabric on the floor, and cut it all out. Phyl sewed the pieces together using her trusty treadle, a sewing machine operated by foot power. The treadle mechanism connected to the arm of the needle, and as Phyl worked the treadle with her feet, the needle arm pumped up and down, lifting the needle in and out of the fabric, which Phyl guided with her hands.

When the tent was completed, snaps and all, it weighed about two kilograms and was big enough for the three of them. A little V-shaped antechamber held their packs and boots. The guy-ropes were very strong and matched perfectly to the weight of the fabric. The tent fabric was water resistant as long as nothing touched the sides during a rainstorm. Over the years, waxes renewed the surface.

Phyl also sewed climbing clothes because store-bought clothing did not last in the bush, nor did it keep the flies from biting and the rain from soaking their bodies. She often made climbing trousers out of old wool blankets, for the natural oils in the blanket made the trousers rainproof, almost waterproof, windproof, and warm. Yet the wool breathed, so the wearer never really got heated in these home-made pants. Phyl generally sewed hers as knickers and then wound puttees around her legs. She always wore a wool shirt and carried extra sweaters. She never put the sweater on until they stopped, because this was when the sweat on her skin would cool and give her shivers. For instance when she stopped for lunch, Phyl would put a sweater on and then if needed, she would also add what they called a "bone-dry." The bone-dry coat was the same canvas-type coat as that worn by loggers, except an extra piece of canvas was sewn over the shoulders and down the back to help with perspiration beneath the climber's pack and as an extra padding against the wooden pack frame. The bone-dry coat also had pockets for carrying a compass, a notebook, pocket knife, and snack foods that would be awkward to get to in the clothing layer beneath. The bone-dry trousers generally did not have pockets, but they were essential when pushing through wet bush as they were almost completely waterproof.

When Don and Phyl began climbing the mountains around Vancouver, people packed their supplies by wrapping everything up in a wool blanket and then fastening and knotting it up with rope or belt. They looped the rope or belt to make a shoulder strap and slung the load over a shoulder. Soon packboards were invented and hikers could have their hands free because their load was fixed to a wooden frame fitted with shoulder straps, which balanced the load between the shoulder blades. Don did not like the Trapper Nelson style packboards then in vogue. He thought the wooden side pieces were far too long for hiking in dense underbrush as they easily caught on vines, salal, or fallen logs. He fashioned his own packboards, tailor-made them for himself, Phyl, and eventually Edith.

The two wooden bars down the side of the frame were shorter than conventional ones. The other advantage to Don's design was that the canvas packs were completely self-contained and could also be used without the packboards, unlike the Trapper Nelson design that integrated the pack onto the board.

∞

In 1923 alone, the Mundays managed to squeeze an amazing number of trips into a single season. Beginning in February, Phyl was the only woman amongst thirteen club members to participate in a snowshoe trip to Mount Strachan (elevation 1455 metres). They stayed overnight at the club cabin on Grouse, where, no doubt, they thawed the gramophone by placing it inside the wood-fired cast-iron oven before playing dance music until the wee hours. As Edith was now two years old, Phyl could leave childminding to Don or her mother on an occasional weekend.

The following month Don led a group of twenty BCMC members to Goat Mountain and returned via the Lynn Valley. In April, Phyl, Don, and club members went to Cathedral Mountain near Seymour Lake. In May, Don again led a group, this time on a one-day trip up Dam Mountain. In August the BCMC annual camp was at Avalanche Pass, southeast of Alta Lake (now known as Whistler). At the time there was no Sea-to Sky Highway, and travel to the area required some planning and co-ordination. The climbers took the Union Steamship from Vancouver up Howe Sound to the dock at Squamish, and then caught the train. The Pacific Great Eastern Railway line, built in 1914, left from Squamish and stopped at Alta Lake, thus reducing the time for overland travel. Once off the train, the climbers rented pack horses to carry their supplies and food the remainder of the way into camp. The two-week camp allowed the Mundays (accompanied by Edith, aged two years), to make several excursions in the vicinity as they explored their favourite Garibaldi Park. They made first ascents of Mount Blackcomb (elevation 2440 metres) on the western end of the Spearman Range and Overlord Mountain (2625 metres) in the Fitzsimmons Range.

Later in the month, after the camp was over, Phyl and Don, again accompanied by Edith, travelled by train to the small town of Hope, which lies at the foot of the Coast Mountains, up the Fraser Valley from Vancouver. From Hope they went by automobile to Laidlaw, where they had arranged to hire pack and saddle horses for the ride through the timber into the Cheam Range of mountains near Jones Lake (now known as Wahleach Lake). There, at the north end of the lake, was a small B.C. Electric Railway cabin beside the hydroelectric dam. Mr. Barr, the operator, gave the Mundays a royal welcome and it was from here that they set up their base camp. They reconnoitred the "Lucky Four" group, so named for the Lucky Four Mine by Arthur Williamson, the mine superintendent. Three of these peaks bore the names of the principals of Foley, Welch and Stewart, a railway construction company that at one time was the largest in North America. This company built the Fraser

Canyon section of the Canadian Northern Railway and many other rail lines.

The fourth peak, also named by the mine superintendent, received its name only after the Munday visit to the area. He named it Baby Munday Peak in honour of Edith's mountaineering experience. Another mountain nearby he named Lady Peak in Phyl's honour. The Geographic Board of Canada adopted Baby Munday Peak as an official name in 1946. On this 1923 trip the Mundays explored the area with an eye to a return trip and during a thirteen-hour climb, made a first ascent of Mount Stewart, reputed to be the most difficult mountain in the range. On the club trip the following July they returned to the area for a successful ascent of Mount Foley.

Phyl and Don had extraordinary and finely tuned abilities to navigate in the bush and to climb in areas where few ventured to go. Their reputation gave Mr. Williamson, the mining superintendent, an idea. He invited the Mundays to put their mountaineering skills into use for the mining industry, and told them of his hopes to relocate the first producing silver mine in the province, the Eureka-Victoria mine, which had not operated for almost half a century. Although its specific location had been lost, the mine site was generally believed to be high on a mountain some thirteen kilometres from Hope. In July, right after their climb in the Cheam area, the Mundays headed to Hope and to this search.

Phyl took photos as Don swung precariously on a rope over a cliff edge outside the entrance to an overgrown mine tunnel. The rocks of the cliff edge showed that the tunnel had been cut right into an open vein of ore. As Don dangled, he used his ice axe to break off samples of rock around the entrance, which he then brought down the mountain with them. The samples that Don collected were assayed and discovered to be a silver-gold ore. The miners acted quickly and within a week or so commenced mining operations. The revival of the mine signalled an economic boon for Hope and the vicinity, and the story of its discovery added to the popular lore about the Mundays.

Climbing with a young daughter took a certain fortitude and patience, although Edith was never much trouble. She had accompanied her parents from an early age, and being on climbs was just a natural part of her life. The rhythm of the climb, of Don's stride and arm swings as he carried her, lulled her and kept her content for several hours at a time. She would hum with the rhythm of his walking. For her mother, this humming was a soothing and sweet sound of absolute contentment, and Phyl never tired of hearing it. Edith knew and accepted the routine of the outdoors. As she grew, Don adapted his method of transporting her. The sling over his shoulder that held her as an infant had soon developed into the specialized backpack, then a larger one, and finally, once she was walking, Edith began to climb on her own. A little at a time in areas free of dense underbrush and on wide trails, Edith and her parents worked on finding the right combination of carrying and putting down. Eventually Edith had her own pair of hiking boots with tricouni nails and also snowshoes for winter walking.

On many of the climbs, going in to Garibaldi, the Selkirks, and the Rockies, the Mundays, like other climbers, used pack horses to carry their provisions. Edith loved horses and as a toddler pretended she had her own. Phyl told an interviewer who asked about hiking with Edith: "She always has an imaginary pack train, she will talk to these horses and pick up a stone every now and again, and throw it ahead of her and call out her horse's name, and tell him to get going." It was this contentment that charmed many in the Munday circle and created a legendary quality to the remembrances of Edith on the trail and at camp.

Phyl and Don began branching out. They were now members of the Alpine Club of Canada (ACC) and through this organization broadened their web of social contacts with other climbers. Unlike the locally based BCMC, the ACC membership reflected a geographically disparate group whose common interest in mountain climbing brought them physically together each year at club camps held in the Canadian Rocky Mountains. Before long the Mundays were not only attending the annual camps but had attained their Climbing Badges for special types of climbs. Phyl later went on to earn the Silver Rope Award, signifying her as a qualified leader on climbs chiefly in snow and ice. Later, with Don, she also edited the *Alpine Journal* for several years and acted on the executive.

Somehow she and Don managed to balance activities with both organizations until 1930 when they broke with the BCMC, because they found it impossible to contribute fairly in two clubs at once. They were never just joiners, but busy and active club participants. For the Mundays, the ACC held the most promise for serious and committed climbers who wished to explore beyond the immediate vicinity of the Lower Mainland and Vancouver area.

Phyl was always conscious of pulling her own weight. As she was often the only woman on the more daring climbs or the more isolated ones, it was important to her that she not be a burden to anyone. She knew that for many men, the mention of a woman climbing with them would be met with grumbling and resentment. Just before the famous Mount Robson climb in 1924, Phyl saw, to her horror, one of the male climbers open the pack of a female companion and take some of the supplies out and place them in his own pack. This deliberate and surreptitious act conveyed to Phyl so clearly the attitude of many male climbers who had little confidence in the ability of their female companions to carry a fair load. Perhaps the man thought he was being kind by lightening the load of another and thus assuming a greater load for himself, but to Phyl this was unacceptable. She carefully guarded her own pack and continued her resolve to prove her abilities. Consequently she outdid herself over and over, and much to the amazement of the men, often carried (without grumbling) a pack much heavier than their own. Phyl was "a strong woman, as strong as any man," asserted renowned Rocky Mountain guide Edward Feuz Junior.

At Alpine Lodge – home to the Mundays for three years – Phyl served lunches and drinks to weary hikers, and in the winter, Don rented toboggans. Don and Edith pose with Phyl's sister Betty, her mother Beatrice; and (possibly) her brother Richard, ca 1925.

8

Living in the Mountains

Weekends were for hiking and climbing. Don's cabin on Dam Mountain served as a weekend retreat, but it wasn't long until they contrived to live in the mountains. In the summer of 1923 local promoters who had purchased much of Grouse Mountain convinced Don and Phyl to partner in a venture to develop and open up Grouse for recreational use. In July, Don reported in the BCMC newsletter that beginning in August, a new trail up Grouse would be completed by "the interests who intend to place a hotel on the plateau." This new route, which Don cut himself, began at the Lonsdale streetcar terminus, headed east to St. George Avenue, past a sawdust pile left over from an abandoned mill, along an old skid road up the open west slopes of Dome Mountain, to the trees at the edge of Mosquito Creek at 935 metres elevation. From here the new trail angled westward toward the end of the existing trail on the bare rocks overlooking the city and continued up above the east bank to the creek. It then zigzagged up the side of Grouse to the plateau. The trail boasted an easy gradient suitable for all foot traffic and for pack or saddle horses, the latter available for rent at trail-head from Don Munday. Don was also in charge of building a cabin, the first phase of the development before a chalet-style hotel was to be constructed. For this work, Don was to be paid five dollars a day.

To be more accessible to the mountain, Don and Phyl moved from South Vancouver to North Vancouver, at 162 King's Road West. It wasn't long until they realized the days could be more productive if they just stayed up on the mountain during the heavy, tiring days of building the log cabin on the edge of the bluff of Grouse Plateau. They lived beside Grouse Lake in a large canvas tent complete with cook stove. The stovepipe angled up through a hole in the canvas roof. The tent bore a wooden sign that read Alpine Lodge, the name of the as yet unfinished cabin. From this tent Phyl ran a refreshment stand and served sandwiches and cool drinks to hikers.

Many weeks went by as Don toiled. When the snow came, complications arose, not the least of which was living in a tent with baby Edith. The heavy snowfalls in the night meant that the Mundays had to set their alarm clock to wake them every hour, so they could get up and scrape the snow off the tent roof to prevent the whole thing from collapsing in. One night, Phyl woke with a start and put her hand up. The tent was practically right down on top of them! Hurriedly they put a wooden apple box over the sleeping Edith, in hope that it would give her air if the tent came down. With great care they squeezed out of the door and gently took the snow off in such a fashion that they did not leave the tent roof unevenly weighted.

Phyl wrote an account of their experience for the *Vancouver Province* newspaper. "Don spent every daylight hour working on a substantial log cabin, while I sawed and chopped firewood, cooked the meals, took care of my baby, scraped snow off the tent (every hour) and helped Don between whiles. The middle of December came with the weather getting worse and the snow deeper, so we knew we must soon move under a solid roof, or be buried under the wreckage of our tent. Even with two friends to help us, the situation was fast becoming desperate unless the weather relented. Part of the cabin was roofed but lacked floor and windows, and the walls were still unchinked. We watched the sky anxiously… by night the mountaintop was enveloped in a raging blizzard. The heavily iced edges of the fly whipped and crashed against the roof of the tent till it seemed the canvas could stand the strain no longer… We worked all that night. The usual five minutes walk to the cabin now took half an hour or more with fifty-pound bundles of floor boards on our backs… The only light was a feeble electric torch… One man laid flooring and one packed it from the tent, while I alternatively helped with both jobs. The other man worked without rest shovelling snow from the tent where my baby was peacefully sleeping through it all." By dawn enough flooring had been laid to bring in their supplies and furniture. They nailed the frozen canvas fly from their tent over the unwalled section of the cabin and then used the cabin door as a sled for the first load.

"Edith thought that the wonderful world of snow must have been made purely for her own pleasure. She thoroughly enjoyed trip after trip from tent to cabin. Her joy relieved the strain on us, for we were all decidedly tired and the trips had to be made. By ten o'clock that night all the important things such as the stove, winter food supply, bedding, clothes and household equipment were safe under a solid roof."

∞

That night, ten days before Christmas 1923, the family moved in to the unfinished three-bedroom cabin. Phyl and Don were thankful to be under a safe and strong roof. But it was cold. The ceiling and inside of the logs were completely white with driven snow and frost, and the spaces between the logs had become chinked with snow. Phyl draped large canvas tarps over all their possessions, and then they lit fires in the big stone fireplace in the main room and the cast-iron stove in the kitchen. As the warmth of the fires circulated, everything dripped. The dripping lasted a long time, and as the spaces between the logs thawed, Phyl chinked them with sacking. They did not lack for water inside for many days until all the snow was thawed and had evaporated.

During the few remaining days before Christmas, Phyl managed to steal some time away from her family. She went down the mountain to the house on Kings Road, changed from her mountain gear, and travelled into Vancouver to shop for Christmas. Laden with parcels, she climbed back up to the cabin. Don cut down a balsam fir for their very first mountain Christmas tree, and they decorated it with their own ornaments carefully packed up the mountain. On Christmas Day, Phyl gave her stove its first real test when she cooked a turkey with all the trimmings.

For the Mundays, 1924 was a notable year, not the least because of their abode high above the city. "We were now out on the very edge of the world, 3000 feet sheer above the floor of Capilano Valley, out where you felt you could look out and face the world." Alpine Lodge served not just as their home, but as a business offering "Meals, Refreshments etc. at all hours. Special prices for members of the B.C. Mountaineering Club and the Alpine Club of Canada." A sign outside the front door listed "hot drinks, coffee 15 cents, soup 20 cents, sandwiches 20 cents, meals 1 dollar." Phyl worked hard at this venture, but during the winter months, with no source of water, she was kept constantly busy melting snow into water to cook the meals and for drinking and to clean dishes afterward. The cabin had no electricity. The wood stove kept it heated, and oil lamps provided light at night. Everything was done by hand, and Phyl and Don were the only hands available. With a young child underfoot, operating the Alpine Lodge was a challenge.

∞

It was in 1924 that Phyl achieved what no woman had done before her: she ascended the summit of Mount Robson, highest point in the Rocky Mountains. Fifty years later Phyl would remember the beautiful windless day and the clear unending sea of mountain peaks beneath her feet. "Its something I shall never forget if I live to be a hundred."

But it wasn't just the view from the summit that Phyl remembered. Robson had a reputation for being unpredictable and dangerous. The Mundays' climb was fraught with danger. Two harrowing incidents on their ascent caused them to fall behind schedule and put their lives at risk. In the first situation one of the guides, Joe Saladana, fell and dropped his ice axe down a crevasse. It was a costly error. To go onwards without his ice axe was too dangerous. Ice axes, as all the party knew, were essential on such a climb; they were used not just for cutting steps, but as support on slippery slopes and as an anchor for dangerous sections. It was risky to proceed without it and equally risky to rescue it.

The second incident occurred when Annette Buck, the other woman in the party, disregarded orders – with consequences that were almost fatal. She was on Phyl's rope in the rear position. In front of Buck was another climber, then Phyl, with guide Conrad Kain in the lead. Kain instructed them to move only one at a time and to drag themselves prone across a fragile ice

bridge. Ignoring these instructions, Buck moved care-
lessly and quickly. The bridge shattered and she
dropped into the crevasse, jerking the unprepared man
above her from his footholds. He too fell. Don and his
companions on the second rope watched helplessly
while Phyl braced herself to hold the double weight
and Conrad Kain frantically snatched in the slack. Kain
knew he could not possibly check the three if they fell
together any distance. But Phyl held them until the
climbers regained their footholds and Kain took in all
the rope.

As a result of these incidents the climbers were in
danger of running out of daylight. When they finally
reached the summit, Phyl and her rope companions
only had a few minutes in which to savour their accomplishment before Kain lead them down and off the cornice to allow the second rope party (which included
Don) to have their own brief moments at the top.

Phyl descended the steep and brittle mountain
face. The climbers were single-file, the rope joining
them for safety. Every movement was like hugging the
edge of a sword's blade, and a single misjudged step
could put a companion in jeopardy. They passed the
slight widening where the next four in their party
awaited their return.

Now Don and the others would ascend. Phyl
beamed at Don, who grinned back at her, and then she
carried on with the other three climbers on her rope.
On they trekked, sliding across the big, broken glacier,
then traversing the edges of the crevasses – those great
gaping cracks in the glacier that were too wide to jump
across and often as deep as the glacier itself. Reckoning

that the path of their ascent could also guide their descent, the climbing party intended to trace their earlier tracks. But soon they found it impossible. While they were higher up on Mount Robson, a snow avalanche – a constant phenomenon at these altitudes – had rolled across the mountain face below and had obliterated any trace of their footprints. Forced now to make their own way, they knew the descent would take more time than they had anticipated.

Following as best they could the landmarks remembered from the afternoon, the four continued on. They arrived at the ice wall – the edge of the glacier. On the ascent, Kain had spent considerable time and energy cutting steps into the wall so the party could climb up onto the glacier and continue towards the summit. To do this he first made a handhold in the ice and then, while holding fast, he swung his ice axe with the other hand, slashed at the surface to make a step, then used that step to stand on. He then made another hand hold, pulled himself up, and slashed away at the ice to make the next step. It was backbreaking and painfully slow work, but there was no alternative. The steps he fashioned in a zigzag as this pattern was safer than a straight vertical climb. Ropes linking each climber to the other provided some measure of safety on the ascent. The same would be true as they used the steps for their descent.

But without the benefit of the tracks of their ascent, finding the steps would be a challenge. As she looked around, matching landmarks to memory, Phyl walked a little off in one direction. *This feels like it. Only one way to find out*, she thought. "Conrad, let me check this place. It fits with my remembrance." The other two came closer and they prepared to take the weight of Phyl's body with the rope. "All right," said the Austrian, as he dug his ice axe into the glacier. If she was wrong, they would have a blind search along the ice wall until they found it, and that would take up more of the precious daylight.

"This is it, I'm sure, Conrad. If you can support me with the rope, I'll see." Phyl turned with a twist and lowered herself slowly over the edge to feel for the first foothold. Linked by rope to their guide – who was now firmly planted to anchor the rope and prepared to support her weight – she suspended her lower half over the glacier's edge, tentatively at first, feeling a bit like a spider floating out on its silken thread, wavering on the edge of nothingness. Then she connected.

"There it is." The first step found. It was not such an easy task, blindly groping for the footholds at the glacier-edge, but she recalled their pattern and regularity and was soon down. The others followed, including Don's party, who had finally caught up to Phyl's. They were now off the upper glacier and on the moraine alongside. Here it was steep going but the ropes were not necessary, so they unroped and started down the rocks, carefully springing from one to the other, in hope that they could make quicker time on solid land. As the dusk settled in, it became slow work and not easy to keep the group together. Smoke from a brush fire somewhere far below on the mountain slopes drifted up to them in the twilight. The acrid smoke stung their eyes and complicated the visibility. Smoke was not what they needed. It was hard enough to see in the twilight. Off to the west, a gathering thunderstorm further obscured their vision. Distant thunder rumbled. Darkness approached rapidly.

"It's just too hard to see on the rocks in this light." Conrad declared as he held up his hands to signal a halt. *I agree*, thought Phyl. *If one person twists an ankle or even worse, breaks a leg, the group will be in jeopardy.* "We will have to remount the ice and hope that once out of the glacier shadow, we will be able to take advantage of all the remaining light."

While Phyl, Don, and the others reharnessed their ropes, Kain went on ahead. Once more he cut steps into the glacier edge. Soon he was back, and they all climbed up onto the lower glacier. Because the dwindling light reflected off the snow and ice, travelling on top of this glacier proved less difficult than fumbling around on the dark rocks. Here they could see the way forward. On they continued, walking as fast as they safely could.

The time was just after 10 p.m. Five hours since Phyl stood on the summit and over nineteen hours since they began the climb from high-camp, and they were still far up the mountain. It was now obvious there was no way they would make it back to high-camp this night.

Now, only part way in their descent, they must stop to rest, but they could only do so in a safer place. The glacier face was too exposed. They needed to get to the shelter of the rocks below it and to a lower elevation. There was no easy route. Phyl, Don, and their companions looked around to locate the best way, but it was slow work as the angles of the ice could no longer be judged with any accuracy. Every move was

tenuous. The light was almost spent, and all around
them they heard the grunting and vibration of the ice
pack. It was not pleasant there in the darkness on the
glacier. Finally their guide made a decision.

"I've found a spot. It's a bit tricky, but we don't
have any other options. We will have to cross a six-inch-
wide ice bridge. A couple of steps farther and then we
jump up – I know it is a blind jump, but trust me –
onto an ice ledge where I have cut a foothold. From
there, you will see the rock ledge below, and that is
where we will spend the night."

By 10:30 all eight of them were on the rock ledge.
As she inched the thirty-five-kilogram pack off her
shoulders and then sank to her knees on the stony
ground, Phyl let out a sigh. "Oh," she murmured and
turned over so she sat leaning up against her pack.
"Who would have thought that it would feel so wonderful just to stop moving forward!" Don joined her.
"What we need now is some food. Do you realize that
it is almost twenty-four hours since we ate breakfast?"

"Yes," Phyl replied. "Eating was the last thing I
thought of, although I did manage a small handful of
iron rations just before that final push to the top. Those
raisins and nuts gave me something to chew on,
although I confess I don't actually remember eating
them, my mind was so intent on the climb. It's amazing
what the human body can do." And then she added, "I
carried a treat with me today for us to celebrate our
climb." She opened the canvas flap on one side of her
pack and pulled out a bundle.

"Oh, I might have known it," laughed Don, point-
ing and calling to Conrad and the others. "Look what

Phyl smuggled up to the summit of Robson." With a smile of glee, Phyl held up her treasure. It was a small can of pineapple. "There is enough for everyone to share," she said. "It's a special treat to go with the rest of our food." Everyone cheered. Now that they had stopped, the climbers began to relax. Hands dug into packs to bring out small stashes of food, and they all shared.

They were at an elevation of 3200 metres above sea level. Clouds hung low all around them on the glacier and on the shoulders and cliffs of the mountain. The night grew bitter and the cool glacier breeze insured that no one could keep very warm at all, but they were thankful it neither rained nor snowed. They huddled together and tried to sleep. Sleep came only in snatches because the mountain noises and their precarious position ensured they could never fully relax. Rolling echoes reverberated as falling ice crashed down from the glacier walls and loose snowbanks shifted in the night winds.

At 3:30 a.m., Kain roused them all. It was still dark, but dawn was quickly approaching. The climbers groaned in agony and pulled their cold, stiffened limbs into action. They felt clumsy at first as they reacquainted their legs with movement, but soon they adjusted. As the light increased, climbing became easier. An hour and a half later the group approached high-camp at the timberline on the southwest face. The guide let out one of his famous greetings, a loud yodel, to announce their arrival.

Herbert Newcombe, who was the cook stationed at the high-camp, had soup, toast, and tea ready for them. High-camp was only a transition. Its provisions were slim and consisted of the basics – Herbert, three tents, and a stove, cooking utensils, and bedding. But this morning the camp was a busy place. The next group had arrived and were awaiting their turn to climb with Conrad Kain and to try for the summit of Mount Robson. The Mundays and their climbing partners could not rest here, so they said goodbye and thank you to Kain, who would remain at this camp to sleep before venturing up the mountain again tomorrow.

At 7 a.m. they continued their descent along the extremely steep route over bare rocks. In places, ropes had been permanently fixed into the rocks to assist climbers. Down they clambered and emerged at Lake Kinney Camp (elevation 2969 metres). Here they enjoyed a good, long second breakfast. But they could not rest yet. They were still on the mountain.

The Mundays tramped down the long and dusty trail to the Alpine Club of Canada's main-camp in Robson Pass some twenty-five kilometres distant. The weather was dry and hot, and the trail seemed endless. Phyl encouraged herself to keep going. They had been through all the dangerous parts, had surmounted obstacles she had never encountered in previous mountain climbs, and had attained their goal – a successful ascent of the highest peak in the Rocky Mountains. This last bit, though, seemed to stretch on forever. The heat from the sun threatened to overpower their exhausted bodies, a tremendous change from the freezing temperatures higher up. On they trudged, and about 2 p.m. they arrived at the main-camp with its dozens of tents, the large cooking and mess tents and the community firepits nestled amid the trees. With the exception of the five hours of so-called "rest" on the rocks the night before, the party had been on the go for almost thirty-five hours, since 3:30 a.m. the previous day.

At last they could stop. Friends helped them take off packs. Word of their return spread quickly, and the campers gathered to congratulate and pepper them with questions. The climbers' throats were parched and swollen. Rest was what they required, and then, slowly, tea and soup would work wonders. As they eased their tired bodies into their canvas tent and onto their eiderdown sleeping bags, Phyl whispered to Don. " Can you think of a better life? This is the best!"

Climbing Robson was the first time Phyl or Don had climbed with professional mountain guides, and it was also the first time they had been on different rope parties. The difficulties they had encountered on the climb had resulted from others' errors in judgment. Phyl and Don were convinced that these situations would not have occurred if they had been climbing together on the same rope and with hand-picked companions they could trust. They decided that they would never again be separated. The more they climbed, the more they melded completely as a team, each so aware of the other's position and intuitive to every move. It was a combination that couldn't be beaten.

For some time after moving into the Alpine Lodge, Phyl persevered as a Guide Captain although she had to travel for two hours down Grouse Mountain (and then back up again) to attend the Company meetings. She stopped each way at the Kings Road house to change her clothes. It was a long trip and a big commitment. She travelled down at dusk and returned in the dark, following the trail through the forest with just the light of her "bug," a candle pushed up a hole in the side of a jam tin. This was her only trail light. An owl talked to her each time she passed a particular spot on the trail. Every time he called, Phyl would answer, he would reply, and she would answer again. Each trip this went on until she was safely out of the woods and on to the plateau. Don always had a lamp lit in the cabin window to guide her for the last part of the trip.

Was it lonely? Was she frightened? Perhaps, but she managed for as long as she was able. Finally, though, it was just too much, and Phyl requested a leave of absence from her position as Captain. With the exception of seven weeks in the spring of 1921 after the birth of Edith, this was her first absence since starting the Company in 1910.

It hurt Phyl to leave the girls and to lose the comradeship. Up on Grouse Mountain, the isolation of her situation struck her in a way she had not considered before. "There must be girls out there spread out on the coast in isolated spots who are also unable to travel and join up with other girls. Yes, think of it, all the small logging camps, the fishing communities, and the mining towns. Surely Guides can come to them, and like them I can be linked also!"

Within months of her request for a leave of absence, Phyl became convinced that she could continue Guiding while on Grouse Mountain. But to do so she must form a new and completely separate Company of girls, not in Vancouver but in isolated circumstances, girls who would otherwise have to give up Guiding, or never know Guiding. In March 1924 Phyl organized and registered the 1st Company of Lone Guides. She registered it initially as part of North Vancouver and then, as it began to serve a much wider base, as a provincial Company.

The cabin on Grouse Mountain became, at 1270 metres elevation, the highest Girl Guide headquarters in all of Canada. Phyl found girls, and they found her. She did not have many in the Lones Company at first, but they were scattered from Alaska to California and into Alberta. Phyl began to pull these girls together with an ordinary letter as a means of communication, but she soon fell upon a better scheme. She started a progressive newsletter that began with a message to the girls from Phyl as Captain, and news and greetings from each Patrol Leader. She filled several more pages – with riddles and information on nature, questions and answers on knots or other Guide work, songs and stories – all illustrated by either drawings or pictures. She added updates on each girl in the Company, including biographical information, so that Lone Guides could get to know each other remotely. Phyl then sent the newsletter in the mail to one girl in the Company. The roll call was their mailing list. Each girl had set dates that she might keep the newsletter before passing it on to the next girl on the list. At the end of the newsletter was a "Post Box" where girls could write little notes from one to another, and so in this way they could also communicate with each other as they passed the newsletter on. Phyl even conducted inspection by reading the girls' answers to questions posed in the newsletter. For instance, one month she might ask: "Is your top dresser drawer tidy enough for Captain to inspect?" Lone Guides were trusted to answer honestly, which they did. One girl responded to that particular question by confessing: "Well, not exactly Capt. but it will be next time."

As the Lones membership increased, the time it took for the newsletter to circulate amongst the patrol members lengthened – especially in the winter. One girl wrote in the Post Box section of the newsletter, apologizing for the delay in forwarding. "I am sorry it's late but it's been forty below here and no one went for the mail, five miles away, for three weeks."

In 1927 Phyl became Provincial Lone Secretary and she now officially co-ordinated the Lones movement over all of B.C. The small Lone Guides Company she began three years earlier had grown beyond her initial vision, and her extraordinary work was acknowledged to be much more than that of a local responsibility. But even with the new title, Phyl struggled to find women who would commit themselves to assisting in the movement. Guiders – those adult leaders in Guiding – were difficult to recruit normally, but to find and nurture a Guider isolated by distance presented extraordinary demands.

It was not until 1931 that Phyl was able to split up the original company into more manageable sizes and register a second one based out of Kamloops. Other companies soon followed. Phyl somehow kept the companies, their captains and lieutenants, and the movement itself centred and dynamic. From the tiny germ of an idea initiated because of her personal situation, and definitely motivated as a solace to her own self, the Lone Guides movement grew and thrived under Phyl's dynamic leadership. She transformed it into an ongoing passion – one that continued long after she and her family moved back to Vancouver and off the mountain.

9

Rising Above All the Others

On a clear, crisp Saturday afternoon in March 1925, Phyl heard cries outside the cabin. She ran to the front door and out on the verandah overlooking the bluff. Yes, there it was, clearly, a voice calling for help. But where? Phyl shouted for Don.

"Someone's hurt, Don. I can hear a call below the bluffs." Pausing long enough to tie up her hiking boots and wrap herself in a winter jacket, Phyl left the cabin and went out on the plateau.

"Hello!" she called.

"Help!" came the reply. "Down here. My friend, he's gone over. I can't see him." Sure enough, there was a teenage boy on the bluff below

BC Archives/E-04938 Don Munday photo.

The main tower of Waddington (elevation 4019 metres) rises to its full glory. "A nightmare molded in rock and ice" is how Don Munday described this mountain, located 300 kilometres north of Vancouver. This view was taken in 1928 from the northwest – and lower – summit, the closest the Mundays ever got in their quest to ascend their "Mystery Mountain."

the cabin. He was in an awful state – scared stiff and panicking.

"Are you injured?"

"No, I'm OK. We were playing and sliding down the frozen slope, but all of a sudden Sid hit a real icy patch beneath the snow. Sid just fell flat down on his back and rolled right off, down the slope and into the trees."

"You just stay still there now. We'll come down to you and get you back up to our cabin. Then we'll look for your friend."

Don arrived with a rope that he anchored and then passed down to Phyl, who stood as far as she dared on the edge of the slope. Receiving the rope, she called to the teenager.

"Here, look up now. I'm sending you a rope. You will have to reach out and grab it. Tie it round your middle and let us know when it's knotted good and tight." The boy did as he was told and then he pulled himself up to a stand and began to scramble up the slope. With the rope bearing most of his weight, he was able to climb unaided to the plateau where Don and Phyl untied the rope.

Rescuing his buddy was another situation altogether. Fourteen-year-old Sid had not been nearly as lucky as his friend had. Not only had Sid gone completely down the slope, but he had managed to slip between the trees and tumble almost six hundred metres farther down to the brink of another cliff. There was no discussion. Don with his weak left arm would be at a disadvantage in leading a rescue. Phyl had her first aid training and could assess the boy's medical condition, and besides, she was strong and in good health.

Phyl went down in among the trees to search for him. She carried one of their climbing ropes and a small pack containing some bandages and a blanket. A toboggan trailed behind her. She didn't know what to expect. Down she went, fearful that she too might lose her balance, but fearful also of what she might find. After more time and patient searching she found him. He was a long way down. So far down she thought she might have missed him as she moved along. His fall had finally been stopped by a windfallen fir tree. There he lay, mere metres from the cliff edge, unconscious.

At first Phyl thought he was dead, but she was able to discern shallow breathing. After a careful examination, Phyl could detect no major bone breakage, and his neck appeared unharmed. But she wasn't taking any chances. She knew he must have a head injury, so they would have to move him with the utmost care. He was limp, a dead weight. Don appeared from above with another rope that he tied around some trees, and then, using the rope to steady himself, he joined Phyl. They tied the other end of the rope around the unconscious boy. Together Don and Phyl dragged him up a slope to the trees. Gently she moved him prone on to the toboggan. Using supplies from her pack, she strapped him and wedged the wool blanket around his head and neck for extra support. Now began the real challenge – somehow to drag the boy on the toboggan back up the mountain.

For three long hours Phyl had to hold the toboggan tail from above as they traversed the slopes, keeping the boy as flat as possible. Finally they got to the cabin and brought him inside, still on the toboggan. Edith was sleeping, and the other boy who had stayed at the cabin to take care of her was now warmed by the fire in the fireplace. He was calmer, but extremely worried about his friend.

"I'll go for help, Phyl. I'll find a doctor and bring him up." With that, Don grabbed the bug light. He would need it on the return trip with the doctor. He ran out the door and down the mountain into North Vancouver to search frantically for a doctor willing to climb up Grouse Mountain to aid the injured boy, whose name was Sid Harling. Meanwhile Phyl knew what she had to do. Leaving him where he lay, she wrapped Sid up in blankets. She then heated water on the wood stove and put the water in empty jam jars, which she placed all around him. She knew that she shouldn't move him, and she knew also that a badly chilled body should not be heated quickly. All the while Phyl checked his pulse and breathing. She was certain that he would die at any moment. But he didn't, and by the time Don returned with Doctor Dyer and a nurse, Sid was breathing evenly and his body was warm.

The doctor examined the boy and indicated that he had suffered a bad concussion. He applauded Phyl's decision to leave him on the floor and move him as little as possible, adding that in his estimation, if Sid had been exposed to the elements any longer than he had, death would surely have resulted. Only the speed with which he was rescued and removed from the cold had saved his life. Both the doctor and the nurse agreed to stay at the cabin for the next forty-eight hours to monitor Sid's condition.

The following evening, the Mundays left Sid in their hands and came down the mountain to attend the local celebrations for the twentieth anniversary of the Alpine Club of Canada, a dinner held at the Hotel Vancouver. Word of the accident had just reached the club, and "cheer after cheer reverberated through the dining room when Mr. and Mrs. Don Munday arrived with apologies for 'being a little late,'" noted the ever-vigilant *Province* newspaper.

The injured boy was unable to travel. Phyl nursed him for over three weeks before he was sufficiently recuperated to handle the trip down Grouse. For her rescue and nursing of Sid Harling, the Girl Guides Association of Canada awarded Phyl their highest honour, the Bronze Cross for valour. She was the first woman in the country to receive this recognition.

∽

Phyl had a busy time on Grouse, for it was only a few months later that she piggybacked an injured teenage girl down the mountain. But the climbing season geared up beginning in May with a little warm-up jaunt to Mount Garibaldi, and then two weeks later she and Don joined good friend Tom Ingram for what Ingram claimed would be "his farewell gesture to climbing." At age fifty Ingram believed his climbing days to be over. Don and Phyl, to humour him, went along. The threesome travelled to Vancouver Island, and by stage from Nanaimo along the Alberni road towards Mount Arrowsmith (elevation 1817 metres). They planned for a four-day trip but completed it in two. This particular journey would set them on a quest – one that might be seen as an obsession – that would last over a decade.

The following month they were in the Cariboo Mountains west of the Yellowhead Pass where they made a first ascent of Mount Sir John Thompson (elevation 3246 metres) and became the second party to ascend Sir Wilfrid Laurier (elevation 3520 metres). From there the Mundays travelled to Lake O'Hara in Yoho National Park for the Alpine Club summer camp.

Two ascents, one of Mount Hungabee (elevation 3493 metres) and Mount Victoria (elevation 3464) stand out for this trip, the latter climb accomplished in a mere two and a half hours up (a new record) and three hours down. But here at Yoho Park, much to their chagrin, they discovered that the existing topographic maps of the park were inaccurate. Trails were shown where none existed. The maps also omitted many important details including the number of lakes on a specific route and the presence of not one, but three glaciers in the area between Emerald Pass and Emerald Lake. Don complained not too subtly in the fall issue of *The BC Mountaineer*. "It might not be out of place to put climbers on their guard against being misled [by the map]." On the section of trail from Emerald Pass, "the conditions encountered contained more concentrated mountaineering than this writer ever wishes to cram into half a dozen trips in future."

Mountaineers who explored and climbed in national parks at this time had only inaccurate or simplified maps to follow. They found the inadequate maps frustrating and dangerous. For ex-Army scout

Don, the lack of information was particularly galling. One of Don's chief delights in climbing was the documentary activity that went with the climb. He and Phyl spent much time and effort carrying in cameras, and later motion picture cameras, to record the scenery and to put together photo-topographic panorama maps of the mountain ranges as viewed from mountain summits and oriented with Don's compass. The Mundays believed mountaineers had a responsibility to forward precise topographic information to the provincial and federal authorities for inclusion in future mapping.

Closer to home, Don and Phyl knew firsthand the limits of topographic maps depicting the Coast Mountains. This mighty range extends from Alaska in the north, down through British Columbia, and south into Washington State. It covers more land than the Rocky Mountains. But apart from the terrain near Vancouver, the Coast Mountains were largely uncharted. Published maps identified only a handful of summits, and guessed at their heights. The few limited penetrations into the mountains produced some documentation, but much was based on speculation. Although provincial surveyors reported features they spied from a distance, little official work had been undertaken. As they explored in the Tantalus Range and around Garibaldi, Phyl and Don cast their eyes northward along the sea of mountains stretching parallel to the Pacific Ocean. They mused about the possibilities for future climbs and wondered what hidden treasures

might be found in the heart of the range. But without
maps to guide them, or manuscript references to follow, could they get access to this great range?

∽

Sitting on Mount Arrowsmith with Don and Tom Ingram
one day in the spring of 1925, Phyl looked through her
binoculars and trained them across Georgia Strait to
the mainland, where, on this particularly clear afternoon, the soaring white peaks stood out in sharp focus
and their full glory. She could see almost five hundred
kilometres along the length of the range. She scanned
carefully, mesmerized by the mountains' sheer magnifi-
cence.

"Don, look!" She handed him the glasses and
pointed across the waters to a section within the deep
white mass. He focussed and then he could see, shimmering above a cloud rift, one fine tall white peak ris-
ing above all others. Quickly he checked his compass
and calculated.

"Looks to me that it's about near the head of Bute
Inlet, maybe just a little east. It's a long way off, must
be at least 150 miles from here. It's magnificent! Phyl,
why hasn't anyone noted this peak before?" Before he
could complete his thought, another glance through
the binoculars answered his question. In the space of
seconds, clouds obscured the mountain and it disappeared.

It was a Mystery, and that is what they called that
elusive peak – Mystery Mountain. Right there, Phyl
knew she had to find it, but with a full calendar of

climbing trips scheduled, she and Don would have to wait until September. In the meantime they would plan an expedition up the coast. Tom Ingram, needless to say, forgot all about his farewell to mountains. This was much too exciting a prospect to miss.

In September 1925, Phyl, Don, Tom Ingram, and Athol Agur boarded the Union Steamship vessel SS *Chelohsin* headed up the coast to Bute Inlet. They took with them a five-metre rowboat with a gas engine, and sufficient supplies for several weeks. After they disembarked at Orford Bay, a local trapper named James McPhee led them up to the head of the inlet to Ward Point. From here the party travelled up a valley and ascended Mount Rodney (elevation 2390 metres) to survey the scene. Looking north, they saw a high prominence – their Mystery Mountain. Don checked the compass readings and calculated the distance to be about sixty-four kilometres from where they stood. Judging by the charts they had brought along, it appeared as if the mountain would be closer to the Homathko River than to Bute Inlet. Perhaps they could access the mountain from the Homathko the next season.

The following summer the Mundays (including Edith), Ingram, R.C. Johnson, and Don's brother Bert again travelled up the coast, this time heading north of Bute Inlet, to the Homathko River. They dropped Edith off to stay with the McPhees. The climbers had five weeks, and they packed in a tremendous amount of supplies over what proved to be an almost impossible challenge of obstacles. They travelled thirteen kilometres up the swollen river in their small boat, then sixteen kilometres by canoe and backpacking, carrying the boat when necessary. They cut a trail the last nineteen kilometres from the boat to their base camp, and then they relayed the supplies, one load at a time. The Homathko River was almost impassable, for the shoreline was flooding and huge debris was crashing downriver. Finding a spot to set up a suitable base camp and relaying supplies took more time than they had ever anticipated. Never had Phyl and Don encountered such unwelcoming country.

One thing was apparent: this land also held an immense quantity of glaciers; Don estimated the larger ones covered forty square kilometres. After one long day scouting out, Phyl became snow-blind from the glare of the snow. Snow-blindness is a painful affliction that lasts for several days. The eyes burn and ache and cannot be opened. Tea poultices relieved the pain somewhat, but for several days Phyl could go nowhere and had to be led by her hand around camp. Finally, one cloudless day they got what they had come for: a first clear glimpse of Mystery Mountain. They also realized that the great glacier, the Franklin as they would name it, came off this mountain, and that the Franklin River flowing from it drained into Knight Inlet. This discovery was an important piece of topographic detail. But now they had run out of food and had to get out and back to the boat.

∽

In late 1926 the Mundays had to make a difficult decision. Their business arrangement with the Grouse

Mountain Highway and Scenic Resort Ltd. had not gone quite as they envisioned. A parting of the ways between the Mundays and the company meant that the family must move off Grouse Mountain. The couple tried to keep a brave face and maintained that the decision to move was based on Edith's need to attend school. She was now six years old. Although she was well advanced in her education thanks to Phyl and Don's home schooling, Edith was ready to spend time with friends her own age.

So the Mundays left Grouse Mountain and the log cabin that had been their home for almost three years. They purchased a tiny frame house on Tempe Crescent high on the Lonsdale slopes below the mountain. "We bought it for the view," said Phyl. "It was such a blow to come off the mountain, we thought that at least here we'd have some of the same marvellous outlook. We see all of Vancouver spread before our feet, and over to Vancouver Island, I can see Mount Arrowsmith. To the west, Horseshoe Bay, The Lions, and the Tantalus Range way in the distance."

It wasn't long until the Mundays were once again in the news. Don's financial situation was made public as he went to court to claim unpaid wages for the 156 days he had spent building the Alpine Lodge. He had not yet been paid the $785 owing, calculated at five dollars per day. For reasons not published, the Court dismissed his claims. It was an embarrassment to have their business affairs become reading material for the city, but losing the court case was also a real financial blow to the Mundays, who believed that they had been taken advantage of and deliberately misled.

∞

Now that she was back in the city, Phyl's horizons for Guiding expanded. When Edith was seven she was old enough to become a Brownie, so Phyl created the 1st North Vancouver Brownie Pack, with herself as Brown Owl. Long after Edith progressed through to Guides and Rangers, Phyl maintained this position, for she really loved working with these little girls. After several years of her Lones work she needed to actually be with the girls, not just in long-distance communication. She eventually became a District Captain and then Commissioner. In 1945 she reluctantly gave up her Lones work at the request of the Guides and assumed the role of Provincial Woodcraft and Nature Advisor. Her knowledge of the outdoors and her dynamic teaching skills combined in these positions.

Munday party crossing a snow bridge on their 1933 attempt
to reach Mount Waddington from the northeast
via Combatant Mountain and Mount Geddes.

10

The Quest for Mystery Mountain

I n July 1927 Phyl and Don, with Phyl's sister Betty, again journeyed up the coast in search of their mountain. The SS *Venture* carried them to Glendale Cove cannery at the head of Knight Inlet, and then they motored the last fifty-five kilometres in their outboard boat. They travelled up the Klinaklini River and went on foot up the Franklin Glacier towards Mystery Mountain. But nature was not co-operating. The routes they scouted to the summit were "guarded by hanging glaciers, icefalls, or rock towers." On the east ridge of the mountain, the danger from rock falls was extreme. All three of them ended up bruised and cut. On one occasion, Phyl averted a disaster when she glanced up

and saw a cavalcade of rocks falling down towards
Betty. Quickly she put up her arm to deflect some of
them away from her sister, but one of the rocks struck
Phyl on her head. The gash bled profusely, leaving her
dizzy, in need of surgical stitching, and in pain. But
with Betty's help, Phyl cleaned herself off in a glacial
pool and soldiered onwards.

While attempting a route on the west ridge, the
climbers made bivouac on Fury Gap (elevation 2900
metres) midway up the Franklin Glacier before they
tackled the remainder of the ascent. Part way up, the
weather changed within minutes. Clouds rolled in,
bringing darkness. Fierce rain and wind, followed soon
by lightning and thunder – wild flashes and fierce, vio-
lent crashes – caught the climbers exposed on the rocks
in a terrifying electrical storm. Phyl had never been so
afraid.

The party scrambled back to Fury Gap. "We had
trouble keeping our lights alight, and it was just pour-
ing down. It's really wild when it's like that, and all
these tongues of fire on the rocks and tongues of fire
on our ice axes, buzzing. Just like a blowtorch almost,
with sparks of fire coming off the tip of my ice axe. We
couldn't throw them away because we needed our ice
axes to cross the glaciers. When we got to Fury Gap we
picked up our frozen tarp and all the things that we'd
left there – film boxes and that sort of thing, and food
and a Primus stove, and we stuffed them into our
packs. Then we went down the slope onto some
shelves of rock – wet, of course, and cold as the dickens
– put a tarp on these rocks, and we three down, pulled
the tarps over our heads, like a lean-to, and we stayed

there for the rest of the storm, until it was light enough to come down the glacier."

∞

In 1928 they returned with Don's brother, Bert Munday. The weather was extremely poor and they bided their time on first ascents of lesser peaks until it was clear enough to attempt their Mystery Mountain, which now had an official name given by the Canadian Geographic Board that spring. Mount Waddington it was now called, to commemorate Alfred Waddington, whose attempt to build a road from Bute Inlet into the Interior in 1862 had ended in disaster. Phyl and Don must have been disappointed, for their original wish had been that their Mystery Mountain retain the name they had always used. The mountain now also had an officially recognized elevation, and the Mundays' estimates of its height were almost bang on. In 1927 a survey crew led by J. T. Underhill had completed triangulation of the mountain and calculated the elevation as 4016 metres. Mount Waddington was now on record as the highest peak entirely in the province, a claim previously held by Mount Robson.

Finally the weather cleared, and the Munday party tackled the mountain, working this time from the northwest. They arose just after 1 a.m. on the morning of 8 July and headed out. After many hours of struggle, they reached a spot where a five-hundred-metre icy slope stretched upwards before them. It was suppertime, could they continue on? The slope was brittle and dangerous. Slabs of ice broke away under their feet. Don cleared and cut steps and handholds and upwards they climbed. The last 130 metres took over an hour. All at once they were there on the top. Surely it was victory at last.

"It was such a satisfaction getting to the top," Phyl recounted. But how crushing it was for the weary climbers as they looked out beyond. The ridge on which they stood, and which they had thought to be the main summit of the mountain, fell away. Across the airy space ahead of them they could see the actual main tower, only sixty metres higher than where they stood on the northwest summit. "We were absolutely aghast. We were so close to the main tower but yet so far. It was out of our reach."

Phyl looked across. The main tower seemed scarcely more than an arm's length away. She would never forget the details. "The rocks of the tower were not all just plain grey; they were different colours, and so beautiful in the evening light." But it was obvious to the Mundays as they examined the summit from their lofty position that the "main tower was a difficult climb." It was now close to 8 p.m. After hours of climbing and little food, the Mundays had to get back to Fury Gap before nightfall. With heavy hearts they retraced their route back down to the camp. They didn't realize that they had reached the highest elevation they would ever achieve on Mount Waddington. Although they continued coming back almost every season for the next eleven years, the prize was not to be theirs.

For Phyl, Waddington was an endless source of frustration, and even Don called it "a nightmare moulded in rock," but at the same time this Mystery Mountain was addictive. Phyl always made it clear that climbing the summit wasn't their only rationale for the repeat visits. Years after their Waddington expeditions, an experienced climber asked her why, with all the opportunities she and Don had, they didn't just conquer the mountain and be done with it.

"Why did you keep going back, Phyl? Wasn't it just wasted time skirting around the big peak and never being successful?"

"Why there isn't *any* one mountain worth throwing your life away on. Our lives were more important than any mountain. If the day wasn't good, we'd go off and do something else. There is a whole new world out there, hundreds of peaks, hundreds of glaciers, and all of it uncharted. It is all so marvellously exciting. Even though we started out on a quest for our Mystery Mountain, we ended up with a lifetime of options, and a lifetime of adventures. Every time – it doesn't matter whether it's storm or sunshine – it's always worth it."

Phyl and Don pioneered exploration in the Mount Waddington area and believed that as pioneers, they should document their activities and also leave a legacy for a wider audience. They knew that it was not just a matter of their own satisfaction and privilege that they climb. They knew that by recording their observations, taking notes and measurements, and collecting specimens, they made important contributions to the understanding of British Columbia geography, flora, fauna, and natural history. This work was their hobby, and they treated it as inseparable from the physical aspects of hiking and exploration. It was the exploration, the need to know and to see and to travel over little-known or little-understood lands that provided the impetus to keep them going.

"We didn't go into the Waddington country just to climb one mountain and run out and leave it. We went in to find out all that we possibly could about glaciers and mountains and animals and nature and everything about that particular area – completely unknown before we went in to it – so that we could bring out the information for the interest of other people as well as ourselves."

Their exciting new discoveries in Waddington territory were worth every hour of struggle, every brush with death. They had many close calls: avalanches, falling rock, rotten snow, fragile ice bridges, unforeseen weather, turbulent glacial rivers, logs and debris, and bears. Phyl was fearless, or at least that is how she appeared to Don and it was how he wrote about her in many articles and stories. It was also how she appeared to fellow climbers, many of whom were in awe of her physical strength and stamina, her level-headedness under pressure, and her natural ability to suss out the one possible route when the way looked blocked.

At various times Phyl coped with salt-craving porcupines, rodents, wolverines, and bears. The bear stories got all the press. Fearless, she charged – more than once – a grizzly bear threatening Don. In 1936, as they paused on a rocky shoulder in a narrow gorge, they spied a young grizzly some distance away.

"Ah, at last, a chance to photograph a bear!" wrote Phyl some time later as she recorded the incident in a chapter of a manuscript she titled "Mountain Memories." The first buzz of Don's movie camera brought the bear's head up with an angry jerk. With teeth gleaming in the sunlight, he bounded straight up a rocky ravine towards Phyl and Don.

"At that very moment we heard a terrific roar close beside us, and there, rushing right at us, was a large she-grizzly with her two cubs, one on each side of her. We were terrified. It is useless to run in a place like this, especially when clad in heavy mountain boots. We stood our ground and waved our arms, screaming and yelling at the top of our lungs. She took a particular dislike to me, and charged straight at me. Don rushed her, to divert the brute's attention, and to my horror she turned at right angles and charged him instead, and there they were, face to face. The bear was so close Don could feel her hot breath in his face. They roared at each other, the grizzly with her mouth wide open, and all hair standing on end like a fighting dog. I was so sure the infuriated brute would lift her paw and tear Don to pieces before my eyes. I grabbed my ice axe and rushed at her intending to hit if she dared lift it... I was fighting mad too." Phyl paused in her writing and then she added: "My knees shook for a long time after that, and do, even now, when I think of it. I doubt if I will ever go through anything like it again, and live to tell the tale."

Throughout the 1930s Phyl and Don continued their endless love affair with the Waddington country. Each season they tried different entry points and covered much territory. Soon the documentation they brought back confirmed that the heart of the Coast Mountains featured vast ice valleys and towering rock summits, undreamed of in either mountaineering or geological circles. The region offered brand-new challenges for committed and skilled mountaineers. The Mundays made first ascents of many major peaks in the area, and on three separate occasions they used skis to make these first ascents and to carry out many of their mapping and natural history observations.

Edith did not take part in the entire Waddington trip until 1937, the summer she was sixteen. That year, the Mundays travelled for ten days up the coast in the *Edidonphyl* (the handmade boat Don built in the basement of their home) from Vancouver to Bella Coola, a distance of six hundred kilometres. They searched for a great peak that had shone out to them while they were on Mount Waddington several years earlier. By hiking overland through some of the most magnificent country they had yet seen, they found and made a first ascent (with Edith), of the mountain they named Stupendous (elevation 2728 metres). Phyl was so proud of Edith – the way she paced herself and handled the ever-changing obstacles of the route. In the deep river valleys, they made their way through underbrush as thick as any they had ever encountered, and on the opposite extreme, they climbed icy slopes and glaciers. Edith's fortitude was a natural inheritance from her gifted parents.

11

Climbing Season

For Don and Phyl Munday the decades of the 1920s through 1940s were composed of two seasons – climbing season and preparation for climbing season. Climbing usually began in June and extended through September. Winter climbs were generally weekend jaunts close to Vancouver and did not require the same preparation as did the more extensive expeditions of the climbing season. In the winter Don concentrated on his writing and submitted many articles for publication. The previous season's hiking and exploration provided plenty of raw material. He also wrote up his notes and researched the history of the areas they travelled into. Don spent a great deal of time corresponding with surveyors,

Phyl cooking a meal, Last Valley Camp below the Franklin Glacier, 1933.

archivists, and historians to learn what he could of past explorations and to locate old maps and writings, which he examined carefully for clues about potential routes or for information about rivers and watersheds.

Don was a member of the International Commission on Snow and Glaciers and a member of several scientific societies. He corresponded with British scientists and passed on his firsthand observations of the huge snowfields, including the massive Franklin Glacier. At this time people were still unsure about whether glaciers moved or were static. Don's detailed measurements and keen observations of specific features, combined with documentary photographs, made an important contribution to scientific understanding.

Nomenclature – the formal naming of geographic features such as rivers, creeks, mountains, valleys, and glaciers – is an important aspect of mapping. As they encountered each unnamed river or mountain, Don and Phyl named them, informally at first, so they would have a workable means of reference. Then, each winter they applied to the Geographic Board of Canada to formally register the names, complete with the requisite information about location, elevation, distance, extent and so on. Most of the names they proposed were descriptive in the sense that they recorded a characteristic in each name. Mountains gained names such as Stupendous, Silverthrone, Dauntless, Whitetip, Combatant, Whitemantle, Finality, and Monarch. Glaciers received names such as Marvel, Scimitar, Ice Valley, Chaos, Splinter, and Portal, while creeks became Fissure, Crevice, Scar, Tumult, and Fury. According to Phyl, the government accepted almost all of the

Mundays' nomenclature submissions. In 1928, to honour Phyl and Don, the Board designated a mountain adjacent to Waddington as Mount Munday (elevation 3505 metres). Naturally, one of the first things Phyl and Don did was to ensure that they were the very first to climb their own mountain.

Photography was a big part of their exploration documentation. Phyl was the principal photographer, starting as she did with a standard no-frills camera she described as an "ordinary Brownie with a click." She graduated to a bellows camera with a good English lens, and then, as she required more detail, especially for her photos of flowers, she handled an Exakta with an exposure meter. For obvious reasons, she did not progress into large box cameras even though their large format allowed a greater range in image quality. A thirty-kilogram backpack was enough weight and bulk without adding such a fragile and bulky camera. They set up a darkroom in their house so Don could develop the film. Phyl generally did the printing, often with Edith assisting. Don also built an enlarger so they could control the entire photographic process and crop, enlarge, and print as they desired.

An important use of Phyl's photography was in public education. She was a popular speaker and developed lantern slide shows to accompany her words. Lantern slides, a predecessor to thirty-five-millimetre photographic slides, were made of transparencies sandwiched between pieces of glass to form a slide. With the aid of a magnifying glass, Phyl painstakingly hand coloured the lantern slides, which were black and white. She soon specialized in detailed and very fine nature photography, for which she received much acclaim. She was in great demand for lectures on the beauties of nature and spoke on such topics such as alpine flora and fauna, mushrooms and fungi, snow scenery, and glaciation. Phyl worked hard to convey the wonders of nature to her audiences and to illustrate what she saw as God's gift to humanity. She wanted people to look beyond the pretty pictures to a more profound understanding of the fragility of nature and the interdependence of species.

∞

Preparing for the climbing season, Phyl and Don made sure that all their camping gear was in tiptop condition and that any rips or weaknesses were repaired. They rewaterproofed their "bone dry" clothing and the tent, renailed and waterproofed their boots, examined pack-boards for weaknesses, and checked over all the cooking supplies. One important task was to experiment with foodstuffs and find some new combinations for meals. Phyl dried apples and other fruits; she planned the menus and estimated the quantities of food they would need for a thirty- or forty-day expedition. The climbers had to carry everything in, so to avoid needless packing it was important to be accurate in estimating requirements. By the same token it was wise to plan for unexpected emergencies, to ensure some flexibility so that rations might extend longer if required. Over the winter they assembled the foods. Many items such as custard powder, tomatoes, peaches, meatballs, salmon, sardines, peas, and jam they purchased tinned. The tins were a natural for rough going because they did not easily break. As plastics had not yet come into use, perishables such as the flour, rolled oats, cornmeal, rice, sugar, butter, and cheese were repackaged into a homemade system of waterproof bags. Phyl melted wax in an old baking pan and then dipped cotton bags in it. When dry, these waxed bags would then be filled and placed into empty four-pound jam tins for extra waterproofing, or tied tight and packed in boxes ready for the boat. Cheese, macaroni, beans, nuts, chocolate, coffee, dried fruits and dried eggs all had to be stored and transported in such a way that they were protected from rain, ocean spray, river water, and humidity. The climbers' very lives depended on the food they packed in, and all care was taken to ensure its safety.

Although some of their climbing companions complained that on Munday expeditions, the food lacked a certain variety after several weeks, Phyl had the art of campfire cooking down to a science. In time, her cooking even gained legendary status. She created a combination of bannock and pancakes known as "panics" and was known to always slip a treat or two into a meal at just the time when a simple thing such as a piece of canned fruit or a raisin-filled tapioca pudding really made the difference to an exhausted climbing group. In 1934 Don and a younger friend, Pip Brock, penned the following limerick in her honour.

> There once was a lady named Phyllis,
> Who did her goldarndest to fill us,
> When we reached the last bite
> We were filled up so tight,
> That we thought she was trying to kill us.

12

Climbing on Alone

At the outset of the Second World War in 1939 Phyllis Munday joined the St. John Ambulance Brigade and volunteered to teach first aid classes. By May the following year, the Provincial Superintendent of Nursing asked Phyl to organize a nursing division of the Brigade in North Vancouver. Never one to decline a challenge, Phyl agreed to this one and accepted an appointment as Lady Superintendent of the 68th Nursing Division. Although she was not a nurse, Phyl knew her way around hospitals and also understood the importance of home nursing, which would be the emphasis in this position. She took courses in air raid protection and civil defence and in turn taught these

In 1982, Phyl Munday, then almost eighty-eight years old, returned to
the Homathko Icefield by helicopter, courtesy of the television show
"Thrill of a Lifetime."

courses along with first aid. She held the position for nine years with a small but effective group of nurses and an excellent doctor. As the war went on, Phyl added to her workload. She also maintained three first aid posts, which took up three nights a week, and did blood groupings. Even Phyl admitted that it was an extremely busy time. She had no car and would not own one until she was in her seventies. All her back and forth was accomplished by walking (for which she was renowned) and relying upon the rather inadequate streetcar service.

In the spring of 1948, massive rains and a melting snowpack caused the Fraser River to flood its banks. Although a system of dikes had been constructed for just such an eventuality, widespread property damage occurred from Chilliwack westward along the huge river delta. Many farms and rural settlements were flooded out, and as the river continued to rise, the province was on high alert. The St. John first aiders contributed assistance. Phyl helped patrol the Queensborough area by walking the shoreline and the dikes to check for weaknesses or leaks.

Finally the river crested. The worst of the damage had been done. Together, Phyl and her sister Betty McCallum spent ten days on flood duty at Durieu at the head of the completely flooded Hatzic Prairie. They travelled by fisherman's gas boat over all the fences and hay fields. Their job was to look after the welfare of the people and to administer first aid as needed. It was to be many days until the waters receded and the rebuilding commenced.

In 1949 Phyl received a promotion, to Provincial Superintendent of Nursing Divisions (Betty would then assume Phyl's former position). The same year she co-ordinated the St. John appeal for North Vancouver, to solicit funds for ski patrols on Hollyburn Mountain. She had seemingly endless resources of energy and commitment. As in her Guiding work and mountaineering, Phyl never did anything half way. She was fully committed and fully participatory.

∞

At the age of twenty-three, Edith fell in love, and in April 1944 she married a Royal Air Force flight lieutenant and soon moved to England. Like Phyl and Don, the young couple shared a love of mountain climbing. By leaving home Edith left a gap in her parents' lives, and this might account for some of Phyl's incredible busyness as she involved herself in more and more activities. During the war, Don went through the motions of rejoining, but his age was against him, as was his disability. He decided to aid in the war effort as best he could, which meant abandoning much of his freelance writing and taking a regular job in the Burrard Shipyards. In 1942 and 1943 he spent some time in Yoho National Park in the Rocky Mountains training soldiers in the intricacies of hiking on snow and ice, skiing, mountain climbing, and general orienteering. Recalling his own experiences at Vimy Ridge and Passchendaele, Don knew these skills would be important and maybe even life-saving.

Don was also in the throes of writing a book about Mount Waddington, which would feature the Mundays' adventures and discoveries from the time they first glimpsed their Mystery Mountain all those years ago in 1925. *The Unknown Mountain* had an English publisher and was launched in 1948, just two short years before Don's untimely death.

Phyl could see Don's gradual weakening, his fatigue and loss of fitness. She knew Don was a proud man, so neither of them spoke of it to others, and she did what she could to take the strain off any expectations others might have for him, especially when in the outdoors with friends. In November 1949 he was admitted to hospital, and six months later, on 12 June 1950, Don Munday succumbed to lobar pneumonia with bronchial asthma a significant contributing factor. His lungs and bronchial tubes never completely recovered from the effects of gassing in the trenches in France.

Phyl was devastated by Don's death. Edith was far away in England, and for Phyl, her daughter's absence made the situation doubly difficult. In early July, accompanied by climbing friend Neal Carter, Phyl chartered a small airplane, and they headed up the coast to fly high over Mount Munday. As the sun shone through the parted clouds, she looked once more upon their favourite country and scattered Don's ashes as he had wished, over the wild white glaciers and snowy peaks.

"I've lost my anchor," Phyl cried out. "With Don I've had the best thirty years. We are a team, and now, I have to carry on without him. I'm fifty-five years old, and I'm not sure that I can do it alone." But do it she did. Phyl continued with the Alpine Club, worked for several years as an editor of the *Alpine Journal*, and for two more decades participated in the club's annual camps. She established herself in what she called "the blister tent" and provided first aid to the tired feet of many hikers. As she eased into her sixties she continued to climb, although on easier and shorter trips. Without Don as a partner, Phyl did not attempt the complicated climbs. They had been such a twosome that even after all her years of serious climbing she could not face these challenges without him. It was just too poignant. Neither could she face continuing in a project they had both been working on for some years, a project very dear to her heart. *Mountain Wild Flowers of Canada* was in the proofing stages at the time of Don's death. The book was to be a showcase of Phyl's exquisite photos of alpine flora accompanied by botanical and environmental information. It was never published.

For years, beginning in her mid-twenties, Phyl suffered from arthritis in her knees. Many nights in the privacy of the Mundays' tent she wrapped cool compresses around her sore knees to reduce the swelling. She often was in too much pain to sleep, yet would get up the next day and continue to hike or climb. Phyl made light of the situation and claimed her condition was only "a bit of a nuisance." Her accomplishments are even more remarkable given this physical condition. But just as Phyl protected Don and assisted him with his weak left arm, he protected her so that only very few people ever guessed at the agonies she went through.

Guiding remained a constant source of inspiration for Phyl. Her responsibilities as Divisional Commissioner for the North Shore skyrocketed as more and more families moved in to the area. Finally, in 1956, the district was divided into two, reflecting the municipalities of West Vancouver and North Vancouver. Phyl retained the North Vancouver responsibility for several years longer, and served as Provincial Nature and Woodcraft Advisor through to the 1980s. In 1985, at Point Atkinson, the Girl Guides named the Phyl Munday Nature House in Lighthouse Park in her honour, an appropriate gesture that made Phyl very happy. She was pleased to have her name associated with an ongoing site to facilitate teaching Girl Guides about the wonders of the natural world.

∞

Phyl went back twice more to Waddington, although neither time did she backpack in as she was used to. In 1955 she accompanied Sir Edmund Hillary, famed for his ascent of Mount Everest, on an airplane tour over the area. Her final opportunity came in 1982 as a result of an article titled "Whirling into Frozen Time" in *Beautiful British Columbia Magazine* about a helicopter trip on to the Homathko Icefield and flying over Waddington. The author interviewed Phyl after the trip and then quoted her in the article.

"Oh, I would give anything to go, and I would go to the Homathko and to Waddington. I think I would just weep if I saw the glaciers… I would love to be able to go in a helicopter so I could be put down on a glacier. I would put on my old boots with the tricouni nails on them, take my crampons and walk around for the sheer joy of it."

As a result of Phyl's musings, an anonymous donor paid for her to take such a visit by helicopter. A camera crew for the television show "Thrill of a Lifetime" accompanied her as she stepped out on to the Homathko glacier for the first time in almost fifty years. She wore her old boots and her Guide hat and carried her trusty ice axe. Although she had made many first ascents, this helicopter trip truly was a "thrill," for at age eighty-eight she was frail from a recent fall and her ongoing arthritis. She was imprisoned in a body that could no longer escape to the mountains.

"If I had my life to live over again, I would step out of these awful old slippers and into my climbing boots and start off on the exact same road... providing of course I could have Don." Phyl saw mountains and all of nature as a sacred trust. "We are only the temporary guardians of the earth and without our respect and love it can't last." This belief motivated her all those years when she could not climb, but could instead describe nature's wonders to others. "I have stood on top of a mountain and seen the breathtaking perfection of the earth below."

Epilogue

Rewarded Beyond Measure

Phyllis Munday received numerous honours and decorations in her lifetime, not only for her mountain climbing, but for her service to others, notably in the St. John Ambulance Brigade and in Girl Guides. In 1938 the Alpine Club of Canada made her an honorary member and later named her honorary president in 1971. She held honorary memberships in the American Alpine Club (1967), the Appalachian Mountain Club, and the Ladies' Alpine Club in England. In 1947 the Canadian Council of Girl Guides awarded her its Beaver, the highest honour a Guider could achieve. In 1967 she was named Dame of Grace for her voluntary work in St. John Ambulance Brigade. The University of

Phyl and Don Munday sit on the summit of Mount Reliance
and look towards Mount Queen Bess, 1942.
"And finally, with all the world at my feet, I will sit exalted
on the summit, and just look, and look, and look…"

Victoria conferred on her the title and degree of Doctor of Laws. In 1972 Governor General Roland Michener presented her with the Order of Canada.

Phyl climbed close to one hundred mountains and made over thirty first ascents, many times being the first woman to reach the summit. Asked whether she thought that she was a role model for other women, Phyl replied in her typical and modest way:

"I don't know what women really thought of me... Because if a person enjoys it and you are strong enough, and well enough to do it, and you can hold your own with a party... then there is no reason in the world why a woman can't do it [mountaineering]."

In 1990, after her death, the following thoughts written by Phyllis Munday were read at her memorial service.

> I Think What Will Happen To Me
> When my old body is finished and dies,
> I'm sure my spirit will come to a place like this:
> A lovely woodsy trail, a beautiful lake, an alpine meadow, a ridge and a peak, for all this had been heaven to me while on earth. They are all God's great gifts to man.
> I will roam, at will, about the alpine meadows, along the happy rippling streams, the placid ponds and lakes that mirror the grand peaks and passing clouds. They will catch the early sunrise, with promise of the day, and later the glorious sunset, the last of light, then the night sky with bright stars and brilliant moon.

My spirit will wander about in the fields of flowers, revelling in their unspeakable beauty – it will pause to wonder at a rare treasure on some secluded spot. My spirit will also be tuned to all bird songs, and calls of little animals who make their homes in the mountains.

I will ramble high on the ridges where grotesque trees give way to heather and the highest flowers. Then I will join the fresh breezes, gain in strength, and rejoice in the rocks and snows of high places.

I will travel all over the glaciers – which I love so well – and the sparkling snow fields, the deep blue crevasses and shining seracs and the steep snow ridges and rock faces. And finally, with all the world at my feet, I will sit exulted on the summit, and just look, and look, and look, and love it, and thank my Maker for the supreme privilege my old body has enjoyed through the years.

My spirit belongs to all of the mountains – for this to me is heaven. Thank God who has made me like this. How privileged I have been, as Don and Edith shared these joys with me.

If I have been able to pass on, to even one other soul, the great joy and beauty God gave me in life, then I have been rewarded beyond measure.

Phyllis, Edith (aged four months) and Don Munday
at their campsite in the Selkirk Mountains.

View of Mount Waddington (left) and the Tiedemann Group from the summit of Mount Munday, 1930.

Chronology of Phyllis James Munday (1894-1990)

Compiled by Lynne Bowen

PHYLLIS MUNDAY AND HER TIMES	CANADA AND THE WORLD
	1801 Alfred Pendrell Waddington (future British Columbia entrepreneur) is born in London, England.
	1802 Ceylon becomes a British crown colony; successive governors will seize vast quantities of "waste" land in the central highlands for coffee and later tea and rubber plantations.
1849 Arthur Frank James (father) is born in England.	
	1857 Robert Stephenson Smyth Baden-Powell (future founder of the Boy Scout movement) is born in London, England.

PHYLLIS MUNDAY AND HER TIMES	CANADA AND THE WORLD
	1858 Alfred Waddington emigrates to Victoria in the Colony of Vancouver Island and publishes the first B.C. book, *The Fraser Mines Vindicated.*
	1862 Alfred Waddington chooses Bute Inlet as the starting point for a road into the Interior of British Columbia (B.C.)
	1864 In B.C., in the so-called Chilcotin War, Tsilhqot'in people, made uneasy by European activity in the wake of the Cariboo gold rush, kill fourteen road builders who were cutting Waddington's road; troops are dispatched and five more Europeans are killed; six Tsilhqot'in are hanged; the road is never built.
1870 Beatrice James (mother) is born in England.	
	1872 Alfred Waddington dies of smallpox in Ottawa, Ontario.
	1883 Conrad Kain (future mountain guide) is born in Nasswald, Austria. The St. John Ambulance Association and The Brigade begin teaching first aid and caring for the injured in Canada.

PHYLLIS MUNDAY AND HER TIMES

CANADA AND THE WORLD

1885
Completion of the Canadian Pacific Railway (CPR) makes the mountains of the B.C. Interior accessible to climbers.

1886
Yoho National Park is established west of Lake Louise in the Canadian Rocky Mountains.

1890
Walter Alfred Don Munday (future husband) is born in Portage la Prairie, Manitoba.

1890
Vancouver is the second Canadian city to install an urban electric streetcar system.

1891
An interurban electric street railway is installed between Vancouver and New Westminster.

1894
Phyllis Beatrice James is born to Frank and Beatrice James on September 24 in the central hill country of Ceylon.

1894
Amelia Bloomer, American social reformer and champion of women's dress reform, dies in Council Bluffs, Iowa.

Canadian Prime Minister Sir John Thompson dies at Windsor Castle in England.

B.C.'s Fraser River floods and causes millions of dollars' damage; diking of the river begins.

1896
Esmée Mary "Betty" James (sister) is born.

1896
In Toronto, George Sterling Ryerson organizes a Canadian Branch of the British Red Cross Society.

1901
The James family leaves Ceylon and goes first to England, then Manitoba.

1902
Frank Richard Ingram James (brother) is born in Sydney, Manitoba.

c. 1903
The James family moves to the western shore of Kootenay Lake in eastern B.C.

CANADA AND THE WORLD

1899
The Boer War begins in South Africa; Canada sends troops; the war divides French and English Canadians.

In Canada, the CPR brings in Swiss mountain guides to promote tourism at its mountain hotels.

1900
Robert Baden-Powell is promoted to major-general after his 215-day defence of Mafeking, South Africa.

The first regular ferry service across Burrard Inlet between Vancouver and North Vancouver begins.

1901
Queen Victoria dies and is succeeded by her son, King Edward VII.

George Mercer Dawson, geologist and explorer, dies in Ottawa.

1902
The Boer War ends with the Peace of Vereeniging.

1903
The North Vancouver Ferry and Power Company takes over the Burrard Inlet ferry service and builds a second ship.

1906
The Alpine Club of Canada (ACC) is founded in Winnipeg, Manitoba;

PHYLLIS MUNDAY AND HER TIMES

1907
The James family resides briefly at Slocan Lake in the Kootenays before deciding to emigrate to New Zealand; enroute they change their minds and decide to settle in Vancouver.

1910
Phyllis James begs the scoutmaster of a newly formed Boy Scout troop at St. James Church in Vancouver to allow a troop for girls too; she recruits her sister and seven other girls and appoints herself Acting Patrol Leader.

After several months Phyllis learns about Girl Guides and the existence of a company in Vancouver; she and her scouts form the 2nd

CANADA AND THE WORLD

unlike its British counterpart, the club permits women to join.

1907
The ACC begins to publish the *Canadian Alpine Journal*, an annual publication.

The B.C. Mountaineering Club (BCMC) is founded; six climbers climb Mount Garibaldi.

1908
In Britain, Baden-Powell's *Scouting for Boys* is published in six parts and sells for four pence a copy; the scouting movement arrives in Canada in the spring.

1909
In Britain, the Girl Guide movement is founded by Baden-Powell's sister, Agnes.

The ACC hires Conrad Kain to be its first official guide in the Rocky Mountains.

1910
Baden-Powell writes to Canada's Governor General, Earl Grey, and asks him to organize Boy Scouts in Canada; the Girl Guide movement follows.

In Canada, the National Council of Women speaks out in favour of women being allowed to vote.

King Edward VII dies and is succeeded by his son, King George V.

Phyllis Munday

Vancouver Company of Girl Guides.

As the oldest girl in her company, Phyllis takes her company to Bowen Island for their first camping trip.

1912

Led and chaperoned by Elsie Carr, a member of the BCMC, and dressed in heavy skirts, Phyllis and her Girl Guide company hike to the top of Grouse Mountain.

1912

King George V grants a Royal Charter to the Boy Scout movement throughout the British Commonwealth; Robert and Agnes Baden-Powell publish *The Handbook for Girl Guides.*

In B.C., the Pacific Great Eastern Railway (PGE) is incorporated; Swiss guide Edward Feuz, Jr. moves permanently to B.C., bringing mountain culture and traditions to Canada.

S.S. *Titanic* strikes an iceberg off the coast of Newfoundland and sinks; 1490 people perish.

1913

At the Empire Day parade in New Westminster, Phyllis meets Amy Leigh, lieutenant of the Burnaby Girl Guide Company.

1913

Guided by Conrad Kain, W.W. "Billy" Foster and Albert H. MacCarthy make the first recognized ascent of Mount Robson, the highest peak in the Canadian Rockies; a Mount Robson Provincial Park is established.

1914

Wearing an ankle-length skirt, Phyllis swims fifty metres in the ocean and wins her badge.

1914

In B.C., Canada's Governor General, the Duke of Connaught and Strathern, inspects the Girl Guides in Vancouver.

PHYLLIS MUNDAY AND HER TIMES

Phyllis's Girl Guide company takes on projects for the war effort.

Phyllis attends St. John Ambulance Brigade classes and earns First Aid and Home Nursing certificates so she can teach these skills to her fellow Girl Guides.

Phyllis's sister, Betty, marries Arthur Richard McCallum.

1915
Phyllis joins the Women's Volunteer Corps to do war work; she also works for the Red Cross.

Phyllis receives her Girl Guide Captain's warrant on May 6; at Christmas her company provides Christmas dinner and gifts for two soldiers' families.

After visiting the BCMC cabin on Grouse Mountain in August, Phyllis becomes a general member; two months later, having climbed two mountains and attended three club hikes, she has proved her proficiency and becomes a full member.

In June, after climbing Cathedral Mountain alone, Don Munday enlists in the Royal Westminster Regiment, 47th Battalion as a scout.

1916
For her first big BCMC climb; Phyllis climbs the West Lion with

CANADA AND THE WORLD

On August 4, Britain declares war on Germany; Canada is automatically in the war; young men eagerly join the army.

1915
The Women's Volunteer Corps is established in Vancouver to train women for volunteer wartime service.

At the Second Battle of Ypres in Belgium, Germans facing a French unit use chlorine gas for the first time; the First Canadian Division is gassed on April 24; Canadian Dr. John McCrae writes "In Flanders Fields" on May 3.

1916
Frederick Banting (future co-discoverer of insulin) graduates in the

PHYLLIS MUNDAY AND HER TIMES

a group that includes soldiers on leave awaiting orders to go overseas to fight in Europe.

Phyllis's Girl Guides present a musical entertainment, "The Posy Bed" at the Imperial Theatre to raise money for "patriotic causes."

1917
Phyllis is elected to the BCMC cabin committee.

In July, Don Munday is awarded the Military Medal "for valour at the Battle of the Triangle" at Vimy; in October he is wounded severely in the left forearm at Passchendaele.

1918
Phyllis is working at Royal Columbian Hospital as a stenographer when she meets Don

CANADA AND THE WORLD

same medical school class as Norman Bethune (future founder of the Canadian Blood Transfusion Service).

In B.C., the troubled PGE Railway manages to complete the part of the main line that extends from Squamish to Clinton.

1917
Canadian armed forces in France are responsible for a major Allied victory at Vimy Ridge in April.

In Canada, the Military Services Act imposes conscription, which divides French and English Canadians; to ensure the election of the incumbent Union government, the bill allows army nurses and female relatives of servicemen to vote.

In Belgium, the Battle of Passchendaele (third battle of Ypres) begins; over 15,000 Canadians are killed or wounded in the assault, which eventually captures the village but brings no strategic gain.

October (Bolshevik) Revolution in Russia deposes the monarchy.

Chief Scout Baden-Powell publishes *Girl Guiding*.

1918
On November 11 the Allies and Germany sign the armistice to end the First World War, which has

PHYLLIS MUNDAY AND HER TIMES

Munday who is a patient there; when he is granted weekend leaves they begin to hike together; Don is discharged from the army in the fall.

Phyllis becomes BCMC librarian.

1919

Phyllis and her Guides attend the first Provincial Girl Guide Rally in Victoria; their company is inspected by the Prince of Wales.

On a club hike with Don Munday on Mount Baker in Washington State, Phyllis senses that Don is in danger and saves him from going over an edge.

1920

Phyllis James marries Don Munday at Christ Church Vancouver on February 4; for their honeymoon they take the ferry to North Vancouver, the Capilano streetcar to the end of the line, and then walk to the west ridge of Dam Mountain to the cabin Don has built; later that month they go to Mount Robson Provincial Park to climb Lynx Mountain and Resplendent Mountain.

CANADA AND THE WORLD

killed 8 million people – 60,000 of them Canadians.

In Canada, all female citizens (except status First Nations women) are allowed to vote.

An influenza epidemic that will kill 22 million people begins to spread around the world.

1919

On a visit to Canada, the Prince of Wales buys a ranch in Alberta.

In Canada, the federal government nationalizes several indebted railways to form the Canadian National Railway (CNR), the longest system in North America.

In Ottawa, Sir Wilfrid Laurier, the first French-speaking prime minister of Canada, dies.

Edmund Percival Hillary (future mountaineer) is born in Auckland, New Zealand.

1920

By order-in-council the B.C. government establishes Garibaldi Park Reserve.

In the United States (U.S.), women are allowed to vote for the first time.

In Ontario, Agnes Macphail addresses the United Farmers of Ontario convention; she will

PHYLLIS MUNDAY AND HER TIMES

Since married women tend not to work outside the home, Phyl Munday becomes a housewife and devotes her energies to Girl Guiding; she organizes a ladies' committee and creates the 1st Vancouver Brownie Pack with herself as Brown Owl.

Phyl Munday becomes pregnant, but contrary to acceptable behaviour she continues to climb and backpack until her condition is apparent.

1921
Phyl Munday gives birth to a daughter, Edith, on March 26; the baby goes on a climb up Crown Mountain with her parents eleven weeks later.

1922
Phyl Munday's father, Frank, dies.

1923
In February, Phyl Munday is the only woman on a snowshoe trip to Mount Strachan; in the following months she goes on BCMC expeditions to Goat Mountain, Cathedral Mountain, and Dam Mountain; the club annual camp in August is at Alta Lake, a destination that requires complicated travel arrangements but rewards them with excursions in Garibaldi Park and a first ascent of Mount Blackcomb and Overlord Mountain; later that month they travel inland to the Cheam Range where three

CANADA AND THE WORLD

represent the party the following year when she becomes the first woman to be elected to the Canadian Parliament.

1921
Baden-Powell receives a baronetcy from King George V.

ACC begins to publish *The Gazette*.

1923
Lord and Lady Baden-Powell, Chief Scout and Chief Guide, visit B.C.

In Toronto, Dr. Frederick Banting is notified that he has won a Nobel Prize for his discovery of insulin; he shares his prize with Dr. Charles Best.

peaks in a group called the "Lucky Four" bear the names Foley, Welch and Stewart after a company of railway builders; the fourth peak is named Baby Munday Peak in honour of Edith Munday, who usually accompanies her parents on these expeditions; another mountain is named Lady Peak in Phyl Munday's honour; the Mundays make the first ascent of Mount Stewart.

The Mundays agree to join a partnership to develop Grouse Mountain for recreational use; Don cuts a trail from the streetcar terminus to the Grouse Plateau and begins to build Alpine Lodge; the family lives in a tent on site until they can move into the unfinished cabin ten days before Christmas.

Phyl Munday receives the Girl Guide Medal of Merit in September.

1924
Doing all the work themselves, the Mundays sell meals and refreshments at Alpine Lodge; due to the isolation of her Grouse Mountain home, Phyl Munday requests leave of absence from her Girl Guide Company; in March, she organizes and registers the 1st Company of Lone Guides and becomes its captain.

1924
In Ottawa, Agnes Macphail and nine other members of the Progressive Party form the "Ginger Group" with members of the Labour Party; the group supports proportional representation, sexual equality, and prison reform.

PHYLLIS MUNDAY AND HER TIMES

The Mundays return to the Cheam Range to make the first ascent of Mount Foley; then they head to Hope, B.C. to search successfully for the Eureka-Victoria silver mine.

On July 29, Phyl Munday becomes the first woman to reach the summit of Mount Robson, the highest peak in the Canadian Rockies; the expedition is guided by Conrad Kain.

1925

In June, Phyl Munday is given the first Girl Guide Award for Valour, Bronze Cross for rescuing and nursing teenager Sid Harling on Grouse Mountain.

The climbing season begins in May with a warm-up jaunt up Mount Garibaldi followed by an ascent of Mount Arrowsmith on Vancouver Island where the Mundays look across Georgia Strait and notice one tall peak in particular; because it disappears in the clouds they name it Mystery Mountain.

In June the Mundays make a first ascent of Mount Sir John Thompson and a second ascent of Mount Sir Wilfrid Laurier in the Cariboo Mountains; at the ACC annual camp in Yoho National Park, they climb Mount Hungabee and Mount Victoria but are dis-

CANADA AND THE WORLD

1925

In B.C., the Second Narrows Bridge is built to span Burrard Inlet and supplement the North Vancouver Ferry service.

The United Church of Canada is formed by a merger of the Congregationalist and Methodist Churches and a majority of Presbyterians.

In Germany, Volume I of *Mein Kampf* by Adolf Hitler is published.

PHYLLIS MUNDAY AND HER TIMES

mayed by the poor quality of the maps available for mountaineers.

In September, the Mundays travel to Bute Inlet by steamer and climb Mount Rodney to view Mystery Mountain.

1926

The Mundays travel up the coast north of Bute Inlet to the Homathko River; with supplies for five weeks they travel by boat, canoe, and on foot; they set up a base camp in country that is wild and unwelcoming; Phyl Munday suffers from snow-blindness; before they run out of food and have to leave, they determine that the Franklin Glacier comes off their Mystery Mountain.

The Mundays leave the lodge on Grouse Mountain and move into a house in North Vancouver; a civil law suit regarding unpaid wages brings them unwelcome publicity.

1927

Phyl Munday begins what will be an eighteen-year term as the Provincial Girl Guides Lones Secretary, co-ordinating all Lone Guides in B.C.

In July, the Mundays take a steamer to the head of Knight Inlet, motor a boat up the Klinaklini River and climb up the Franklin Glacier towards Mystery Mountain; an injury from falling

CANADA AND THE WORLD

1926

The Imperial Conference issues the Balfour Declaration, which declares that Britain and the Dominions are constitutionally equal in status.

In Canada, a scandal forces Prime Minister William Lyon Mackenzie King to ask for the dissolution of Parliament, but Governor General Viscount Byng refuses; King resigns and Arthur Meighen succeeds him only to be defeated three months later in a general election; King becomes prime minister again.

1927

The Garibaldi Park Act, introduced by B.C. Minister of Lands, Duff Pattullo, the year before, passes into law; the boundaries of the park will be extended several times.

A survey crew led by J.T. Underhill completes triangulation of Mystery Mountain and confirms that it is the highest peak entirely in B.C.

PHYLLIS MUNDAY AND HER TIMES

CANADA AND THE WORLD

rock does not deter Phyl Munday; they bivouac at Fury Gap during a sudden storm.

1928
The Mundays succeed in climbing the northwest summit of Mystery Mountain, which has been named Mount Waddington by the Geographic Board of Canada; although they will come back every season for the next eleven years, the Mundays will never reach the summit, but they will explore and document the area for other people's use.

In recognition of their contribution to the naming and registering of mountains, glaciers, rivers, creeks, and valleys, the Geographic Board of Canada designates a peak adjacent to Mount Waddington as Mount Munday.

Phyl Munday begins a two-year term as Girl Guide District Commissioner, North Vancouver.

1929
Phyl Munday's mother, Beatrice, dies.

1928
The Supreme Court of Canada says women cannot be senators because they are not "persons."

West Coast painter Emily Carr exhibits her work in Central Canada and establishes herself as a major artist.

1929
Lord Baden-Powell is elevated to the British peerage and becomes 1st Baron Baden-Powell of Gilwell.

The Imperial Privy Council declares Canadian women are legally "persons" and eligible to sit in the Canadian Senate.

PHYLLIS MUNDAY AND HER TIMES

CANADA AND THE WORLD

With the collapse of the U.S. Stock Exchange in October, the ten-year-long Great Depression begins.

1930
The Mundays end their membership in the BCMC so they can devote all their energies to the ACC.

1930
In B.C., the Second Narrows Bridge has not replaced the North Vancouver Ferry service because it is too far to drive to get to it and because it has to open for ships to pass through frequently; a log barge runs into the bridge and destroys it.

1931
Phyl Munday begins a fourteen-year term as Brown Owl to the 1st North Vancouver Brownie Pack.

1933
The Mundays are the first climbers to reach the summit of Combatant Mountain.

1933
Adolf Hitler is appointed Chancellor of Germany.

1934
Conrad Kain dies in Cranbrook, B.C.

1935
Baron and Baroness Baden-Powell visit B.C.

1936
The Mundays are the first climbers to reach the summit of Silverthrone Mountain;; they encounter four grizzly bears, one of which charges them; Phyl Munday saves her husband by brandishing an ice axe.

1936
Americans Fritz Wiessner and William House are the first climbers to reach the summit of Mount Waddington.

King George V dies and is succeeded by the Prince of Wales,

PHYLLIS MUNDAY AND HER TIMES	CANADA AND THE WORLD
	who becomes King Edward VIII; the new King abdicates in favour of his brother, King George VI.

1937
The Mundays travel up the coast in their own boat, *Edidonphyl*, with their daughter, who stays with them for the entire expedition for the first time; they make a first ascent of Stupendous Mountain.

1938
Phyl Munday becomes an honorary member of the ACC; she and Don have been attending ACC annual camps and have edited the *Canadian Alpine Journal*; Phyl Munday has won the club's Silver Rope Award.

1938
Funded by the Guinness Brewing Company, which has real estate holdings on the North Shore of Burrard Inlet, Vancouver's Lions Gate Bridge opens.

1939
In response to the declaration of war, Phyl Munday joins the St. John Ambulance Brigade and volunteers to teach first aid classes.

1939
In September, the Second World War begins when Germany invades Poland; Britain and Canada declare war on Germany.

1940
At the request of the provincial superintendent of nursing, Phyl Munday organizes a nursing division of the St. John Ambulance Brigade and becomes Lady Superintendent of the 68th Nursing Division.

1940
Winston Churchill becomes prime minister of Great Britain.

Future Canadian prime minister John Diefenbaker is elected to the House of Commons for the first time.

1941
The Mundays are the first to reach the summit of Mount Grenville.

1941
Baron Baden-Powell dies in Nyeri, Kenya.

PHYLLIS MUNDAY AND HER TIMES

CANADA AND THE WORLD

On December 7, Japanese planes attack Pearl Harbor, an American naval base in Hawaii; the U.S. declares war on Japan and Germany.

1942
The Mundays are to the first to reach the summit of Mount Queen Bess.

1942
The U.S. and Canada forcibly move Japanese citizens from the west coast of North America.

1943
For the second year running, Don Munday trains soldiers in hiking on snow and ice, skiing, mountain climbing, and orienteering in Yoho National Park.

1943
Due to increased traffic caused by the War, the North Vancouver ferry system has its busiest year.

1944
Edith Munday marries and moves to England.

1944
The D-Day invasion of Normandy by the Allies under the command of General Eisenhower begins the liberation of Europe on June 6.

1945
Phyl Munday begins a two-year term as District Captain, North Vancouver Girl Guides.

1945
Germany surrenders on May 8; Canada is one of the fifty signatories to the United Nations (UN) Charter on June 26; the U.S. drops two atomic bombs on Japan on August 6 and 9; Japan surrenders on September 2.

1946
Phyl Munday begins a five-year term as Captain of the 1st Vancouver Sea Rangers.

The Mundays are the first to reach the summit of Mount Reliance.

1946
Winston Churchill uses the term "Iron Curtain" to describe the alienation between the Eastern Bloc and the West that is developing into the Cold War.

1947

Phyl Munday receives the Canadian Council of Girl Guides Beaver Award, the highest honour a Guider can achieve.

1948

During the Fraser River flood, Phyl Munday patrols the river bank and dikes of the Queensborough area; when the river crests, she and her sister, Betty, spend ten days on flood duty at Durieu on the Hatzic Prairie patrolling by boat for people in need of help.

Don Munday's book *The Unknown Mountain* is launched.

1949

Phyl Munday is North Vancouver Girl Guide Division Commissioner and becomes Provincial Superintendent of Nursing Divisions for the St. John Ambulance; she coordinates fundraising.

A weak and tired Don Munday is admitted to hospital.

1950

Don Munday dies in Vancouver from lobar pneumonia aggravated by the effects of having been gassed during the First World War; his wife scatters his ashes from a small airplane over Mount Munday.

1948

Ceylon gains independence from Britain and joins the Commonwealth.

B.C. is on high alert when the Fraser River floods; the high waters cause $15 million worth of damage.

1949

Elen Henderson, becomes the first Canadian fashion designer to be known internationally; included in her work are uniforms for Girl Guides and Brownies.

1950

North Korea invades South Korea; the UN mounts a police action; Canada sends troops.

PHYLLIS MUNDAY AND HER TIMES

CANADA AND THE WORLD

1952
Forty years after incorporation, the PGE Railway finally reaches Prince George, B.C..

King George VI dies and is succeeded by his daughter, Queen Elizabeth II.

1953
Edmund Hillary and Tenzing Norgay are the first men to reach the top of Mount Everest, the highest mountain in the world; Hillary is knighted by Queen Elizabeth II.

1955
When Sir Edmund Hillary visits B.C., Phyl Munday accompanies him on an airplane tour of the Mount Waddington area.

Phyl Munday is commandant at the Girl Guides' first All Canada Adventure Camp at Lake O'Hara in Yoho National Park.

1957
Phyl Munday begins another term (three-year) as North Vancouver Girl Guide Division Commissioner.

1958
In B.C., an engineering mistake causes the partially completed span of the new Second Narrows Bridge over Burrard Inlet to collapse, killing eighteen and injuring twenty; the North Vancouver ferry system closes.

PHYLLIS MUNDAY AND HER TIMES

CANADA AND THE WORLD

1960
Following the assassination of her husband, Ceylon's Sirimavo Ratwatte Dias Bandaranaike becomes the world's first female prime minister.

In B.C., the Second Narrows Bridge opens.

1961
In Canada, Saskatchewan premier Tommy Douglas calls a special session of the legislature to enact medicare; he resigns as premier before the legislation is passed and goes to Ottawa as head of the newly formed New Democratic Party.

1962
Although she is sixty-eight years old, Phyl Munday begins a long term as Woodcraft Adviser for the B.C. Girl Guides.

1962
B.C. Electric Railway Company is taken over by the provincial government and becomes the B.C. Hydro and Power Authority.

1964
In B.C., at Alta Lake adjacent to the northwest boundary of Garibaldi Park, a ski resort opens on Whistler Mountain.

1965
The extent of the Coast Mountains of B.C. is revealed when climber Dick Culbert writes *A Climber's Guide to the Coastal Range of British Columbia*.

PHYLLIS MUNDAY AND HER TIMES

1967
The St. John Ambulance honours Phyl Munday by naming her Dame of Grace, and the American Alpine Club gives her an honorary membership.

1971
Phyl Munday becomes Honorary President of the ACC.

1972
Dick James (brother) dies.

Governor General Roland Michener presents Phyl Munday with the Order of Canada.

1975
Phyl Munday receives the Girl Guide Long Service Award in May.

1982
Accompanied by a television camera crew for "Thrill of a Lifetime," Phyl Munday helicopters over Mount Waddington and lands on the Homathko Icefield.

1985
Phyl Munday Nature House is opened by the Girl Guides in Lighthouse Park, Point Atkinson, West Vancouver.

CANADA AND THE WORLD

1967
Canada celebrates the 100th anniversary of Confederation; Expo 67 opens in Montreal; French President Charles De Gaulle visits Canada and shouts *"Vive le Québec libre!"* during an outdoor speech at Montreal's City Hall.

1972
The name of Ceylon changes to Sri Lanka.

1976
In Quebec, the separatist Parti Québécois is elected under the leadership of Réne Lévesque.

PHYLLIS MUNDAY AND HER TIMES

1990
Phyllis Munday dies on April 11 at the age of ninety-five.

The Girl Guides establish the Phyl Munday Environmental Fund.

1997
Edith Munday dies.

1998
Canada Post issues the Phyllis Munday stamp in their Legendary Canadians stamp series to honour her many years of service with the Girl Guides of B.C. and her accomplishments in mountaineering and nature photography.

The Alpine Club of Canada sponsors the Grand Prize at the Banff Mountain Book Festival and designates it the Phyllis and Don Munday Award.

CANADA AND THE WORLD

1994
In B.C. the bridge over Burrard Inlet at the Second Narrows is renamed the Ironworkers Memorial Second Narrows Crossing to honour the men who died in 1958 while building it.

1999
The B.C. government officially apologizes for the hanging of the Tsilhqot'in' men in the aftermath of the "Chilcotin War" in 1864.

2002
The United Nations designates 2002 as UN International Year of Mountains.

Sources Consulted

Archival Records

Phyllis and Don Munday: diaries, correspondence, manuscripts, photographs, films and oral reminiscences. British Columbia Archives.

Vancouver District, Girl Guides of Canada records. Guide House, Vancouver.

North Vancouver Girl Guide Archives, Girl Guides of Canada, Vancouver.

Girl Guides of Canada. British Columbia Council. British Columbia Archives.

British Columbia Mountaineering Club fonds. British Columbia Mountaineering Club, Vancouver.

Phyllis and Don Munday photographs. North Vancouver Museum and Archives.

Walter Alfred Don Munday fonds. Museum of the Royal Westminster Regiment.

Published Works
Published Articles by Phyllis Munday:
"First Ascent Of Mount Robson By Lady Members," *Canadian Alpine Journal*, 1924.

"To Mount Waddington with Hillary," *Canadian Alpine Journal*, 1956.

"Wild Animals." *Vancouver Province*, 6 November 1927.

"A Pioneer Homemaker 'Mid Mountaintop Snows," *Vancouver Province*, 29 December 1927.

"Miss Dennis [a pig]," *Vancouver Province*, 20 February 1928.

Other Publications:

The B.C. Mountaineer, (1923 – 1930 consulted) newsletter of the British Columbia Mountaineering Club.

Canadian Alpine Journal, (1920 – 1950 consulted), publication of the Alpine Club of Canada.

Smith, Cyndi. *Off the Beaten Track*. Jasper: Coyote Books, 1989.

Munday, Don. *The Unknown Mountain*. London: Hodder and Stoughton, 1948.

Munday, Don. *The Unknown Mountain*. Expanded edition including essay "Behind the Unknown Mountain" by Angus. M. Gunn. Lake Louise: Coyote Books, 1993.

Munday, Don. *Mount Garibaldi Park, Vancouver's Alpine Playground*. Cowan and Brook House Printers, 1922.

Brookhouse, A.A. *A 'Hike' Up Grouse Mountain. The Experiences of an Unwilling Tenderfoot on his Birthday Jaunt*. Vancouver, 1926.

Leslie, Susan. *In the Western Mountains, Early Mountaineering in British Columbia*. Sound Heritage Volume VIII, Victoria: Provincial Archives of British Columbia, 1980.

Media:

"Our Pioneers and Neighbours: Phyllis Munday." Television interview with Olga Ruskin, Cable West, 1982.

Vancouver Province newspaper, Vancouver.

Daily Colonist newspaper, Victoria.

Guiding remained a lifelong passion for Phyllis Munday,
seen here at Guide Camp in 1955 at the age of sixty.

Index

Note: Page numbers in italics indicate photographs

Agur, Athol, 106
Alaska (state of), 94, 104
Alberta (province of), 94, 147
Alouette Lake, 50
Alouette River, 50
Alpine Club of Canada (ACC), 37, 60, 76, 77, 83, 91, 102, 129-131, 142, 143, 148, 150, 153, 159
Alpine Lodge, *66*, *78*, 80-83, 93, 108, 149
Alta Lake (Whistler), 72, 73, 148, 158
American Alpine Club, 133, 159
Appalachian Mountain Club, 133
Arrow Lake, 4
Arrowsmith, Mount, 102, 105, 108, 150
Avalanche Pass, 72

B.C. Electric Railway, 21, 38, 73, 141, 158
The B.C. Mountaineer (newsletter), 57, 103
B.C. Mountaineering Club (BCMC), *xx*, 20, 35-40, 47, 48, 58, 64, 68, 72, 76, 77, 79, 83, 143-148, 153
Baby Munday Peak, 74, 149
Baden-Powell, Agnes, 12, 14, 62, 143, 144
Baden-Powell, Robert, 11, 12, 14, 139, 142-144, 146, 148, 152-154
Baker, Mount, 45, 53, 147
Beautiful British Columbia Magazine, 131
Bella Coola, 118

Berg Lake, xvii, 59
Bishop's Beach, 67
Blackcomb, Mount 73, 149
Blanshard, Mount, *42*, 50-52
bloomers. *See* Munday, Phyllis, clothing for hiking and climbing
Boy Scouts, 11, 12, 21, 22, 27, 139, 143, 144
Britannia Range, 67
britches. *See* Munday, Phyllis, clothing for hiking and climbing
Brockton Point (Stanley Park), 6, 7
Brownies (Girl Guides), 61, 62
Buck, Annette, 84, 85
Burnaby, 22, 25, 40
Burrard Inlet, 5, 8, 19, 142, 150, 154, 157, 160
Bute Inlet, 105, 106, 113, 140, 151

California (state of), 94
Canadian Alpine Journal, 76, 129, 143, 154
Canadian National Railway (CNR), 59, 147
Canadian Northern Railway, 74
Canadian Pacific Railway (CPR), 2, 4, 59, 141
Canadian Red Cross, 15, 145
Capilano River (and Valley), 19, 20, 83
Cariboo Mountains, 67, 103, 150
Carr, Elsie, 20, 21, 35, 144
Carter, Neal, 38, 129
Cathedral Mountain, 38, 48, 72, 145, 148
Ceylon, 2, 6, 139, 141, 142, 156, 158, 159
Cheam Range, 67, 73, 74, 148, 150
Chilliwack River, 39, 127

165

Printed in August 2002
at Marc Veilleux imprimeur,
Boucherville (Québec).